A Hundred VILLANELLES

A Hundred BLOGATELLES

Copyright © 2017 by Martin Bidney
Dialogic Poetry Press
Vestal, New York

All Rights Reserved

ISBN 13: 9781548296544
ISBN 10: 1548296546

Printed in the United States of America

Available from Amazon at
http://www.amazon.com/dp/

A Hundred VILLANELLES

A Hundred BLOGATELLES

Martin Bidney

Dialogic
Poetry
Press

VOLUME X IN THE SERIES:
EAST–WEST BRIDGE BUILDERS

Copyright © 2017 by Martin Bidney
Dialogic Poetry Press
Vestal, New York

All Rights Reserved

ISBN 13: 978-1548296544
ISBN 10: 1548296546

Printed in the United States of America

Available from Amazon at
http://www.amazon.com/dp/1548296546

The author dedicates his poems and dialogues to friends who have kindly read some of them:

Shahid Alam

Grace Cavalieri

Anni Johnson

Johanna Masters

Katharina Mommsen

Zoja Pavlovskis

Marina Zalesski

CONTENTS

Introduction	**xvii**
Thoughts on "A slender veil, a tender trance"	2
1 A slender veil, a tender trance	**3**
Thoughts on "The planet on creation day"	4
2 The planet on creation day	**5**
Thoughts on "A cinch, a snap, when we've a knack"	6
3 A cinch, a snap, when we've a knack	**7**
Thoughts on "Form is the way we hold our art"	8
4 Form is the way we hold our art	**9**
Thoughts on "Computer update—change at hand"	10
5 Computer update—change at hand	**11**
Thoughts on "To the extent that love allows"	12
6 To the extent that love allows	**13**
Thoughts on "An avian poet sings at four"	14
7 An avian poet sings at four	**15**
Thoughts on "How place-like our container, Time"	16
8 How place-like our container, Time	**17**

Thoughts on "The giant cat will govern fate"   *18*
    9 The giant cat will govern fate   **19**

Thoughts on "The thunder beauty first may shock"   *20*
    10 The thunder beauty first may shock   **21**

Thoughts on "The quiet which at night will come"   *22*
    11 The quiet which at night will come   **23**

Thoughts on "When light and silent time arrived"   *24*
    12 When light and silent time arrived   **25**

Thoughts on "Chance object—pebble near the deep"   *26*
    13 Chance object—pebble near the deep   **27**

Thoughts on "For spectrum-sexuality"   *28*
    14 For spectrum-sexuality   **29**

Thoughts on "Let novel art-style rise in you"   *30*
    15 Let novel art-style rise in you   **31**

Thoughts on "A spectrum-length hate, love attain"   *32*
    16 A spectrum-length hate, love attain   **33**

Thoughts on "How brief a time have I to say"   *34*
    17 How brief a time have I to say   **35**

Thoughts on "The science mind, the will to verse"   *36*
    18 The science mind, the will to verse   **37**

Thoughts on "How fine to feel you needn't bow"   *38*
    19 How fine to feel you needn't bow   **39**

Thoughts on "I thank you, kind electric fan"   *40*
    20 I thank you, kind electric fan   **41**

Thoughts on "Each moment's matter I can mold"   *42*
    21 Each moment's matter I can mold   **43**

Contents ix

Thoughts on "In value realms inventive be"   44
22 In value realms inventive be   45

Thoughts on "Another villaneller-man"   46
23 Another villaneller-man   47

Thoughts on "The vasty volume I peruse"   48
24 The vasty volume I peruse   49

Thoughts on "A spectrum ethic shall we state?   50
25 A spectrum ethic shall we state?   51

Thoughts on "The light through gauzy draping glows"   52
26 The light through gauzy draping glows   53

Thoughts on "The coffee speeds my breathing up"   54
27 The coffee speeds my breathing up   55

Thoughts on "When Blake was dying, loud he sang"   56
28 When Blake was dying, loud he sang   57

Thoughts on "What made the world's unmanifest"   58
29 What made the world's unmanifest   59

Thoughts on "Had fear of silence never cried"   60
30 Had fear of silence never cried   61

Thoughts on "My life shows naught has higher claim"   62
31 My life shows naught has higher claim   63

Thoughts on "A single villanelle, no more"   64
32 A single villanelle, no more   65

Thoughts on "We cheer achievers apt at sport"   66
33 We cheer achievers apt at sport   67

Thoughts on "Who love sweet tone shall never die"   68
34 Who love sweet tone shall never die   69

Thoughts on "The dark is not the Nil at all"   70
   35 The dark is not the Nil at all   71

Thoughts on "You need to change your name within"   72
   36 You need to change your name within   73

Thoughts on "Indignant ire is anger all the same"   74
   37 Indignant ire is anger all the same   75

Thoughts on "Of subject-verb the structure's been around"   76
   38 Of subject-verb the structure's been around   77

Thoughts on "The underwater mind is ocean-wide"   78
   39 The underwater mind is ocean-wide   79

Thoughts on "How are you feeling now, resistless dream?"   80
   40 How are you feeling now, resistless dream?   81

Thoughts on "A pray'r, disease of will; a creed, of mind?"   82
   41 A pray'r, disease of will; a creed, of mind?   83

Thoughts on "To sing in verse for children evermore"   84
   42 To sing in verse for children evermore   85

Thoughts on "Had not the note in thrilliance thralled"   86
   43 Had not the note in thrilliance thralled   87

Thoughts on "A revelation of transcendent things"   88
   44 A revelation of transcendent things   89

Thoughts on "For me who am alive the duty stands"   90
   45 For me who am alive the duty stands   91

Thoughts on "To Essence call an opening your Guest"   92
   46 To Essence call an opening your Guest   93

Contents   xi

Thoughts on "To read in horoscope and see in sky"   94
47 To read in horoscope and see in sky   95

Thoughts on "Coordinate each deep-drawn breath of air"   96
48 Coordinate each deep-drawn breath of air   97

Thoughts on "You've noticed in my float-sway reverie"   98
49 You've noticed in my float-sway reverie   99

Thoughts on "If you envision an epiphany"   100
50 If you envision an epiphany   101

Thoughts on "My freedom will its rival not have bested"   102
51 My freedom will its rival not have bested   103

Thoughts on "The marvel of the writing life unmarred"   104
52 The marvel of the writing life unmarred   105

Thoughts on "No star's outvoted in the lighted sky"   106
53 No star's outvoted in the lighted sky   107

Thoughts on "Devotion is reliant on a vow"   108
54 Devotion is reliant on a vow   109

Thoughts on "For circle-world each look's an upward ray"   110
55 For circle-world each look's an upward ray   111

Thoughts on "Where vigor's matched with rigor would I dwell"   112
56 Where vigor's matched with rigor would I dwell   113

Thoughts on "A triumph in the battle that you wage"   114
57 A triumph in the battle that you wage   115

Thoughts on "The dead are blessed who at night return" — *116*

58 The dead are blessed who at night return — **117**

Thoughts on "What happened to the people made like me" — *118*

59 What happened to the people made like me — **119**

Thoughts on "We Shakespeare call immortal, but he's dead" — *120*

60 We Shakespeare call immortal, but he's dead. — **121**

Thoughts on "When I have died and you, my friend, shall see" — *122*

61 When I have died and you, my friend, shall see — **123**

Thoughts on "The root of 'random' run; the 'chance' root—fall" — *124*

62 The root of "random"—*run*; the "chance" root—*fall* — **125**

Thoughts on "Sub—up to; limen—limit, threshold, sill" — *126*

63 *Sub*—up to; *limen*—limit, threshold, sill — **127**

Thoughts on "Spread wealth. The unaware can't ask for alms" — *128*

64 Spread wealth. The unaware can't ask for alms — **129**

Thoughts on "In growing old I readily forget" — *130*

65 In growing old I readily forget — **131**

Thoughts on "'Tween poem and psychosis, I contend" — *132*

66 'Tween poem and psychosis, I contend — **133**

Contents xiii

Thoughts on "To be a friend and daily offer aid"   *134*
  67 To be a friend and daily offer aid   **135**

Thoughts on "A clever way to complicate the mode"   *136*
  68 A clever way to complicate the mode   **137**

Thoughts on "With crisp attack in clicking touch of keys"   *138*
  69 With crisp attack in clicking touch of keys   **139**

Thoughts on "Muhammad likened milk to knowledge high"   *140*
  70 Muhammad likened milk to knowledge high   **141**

Thoughts on "False Falstaff, Hammy Hamlet, shall I say?"   *142*
  71 False Falstaff, Hammy Hamlet, shall I say?   **143**

Thoughts on "Of bards to whom we most attached have grown"   *144*
  72 Of bards to whom we most attached have grown   **145**

Thoughts on "Of many-voicéd ocean Homer sings"   *146*
  73 Of many-voicéd ocean Homer sings: **147**

Thoughts on "The female sprite that chanted e-mailed lines"   *148*
  74 The female sprite that chanted e-mailed lines   **149**

Thoughts on "Should I, upon awaking, try to say"   *150*
  75 Should I, upon awaking, try to say   **151**

Thoughts on "Converse in iamb and pentameter"	152
76 Converse in iamb and pentameter	**153**
Thoughts on "The dog that shepherded the waves that sped to shore"	154
77 The dog that shepherded the waves that sped to shore	**155**
Thoughts on "When Rumi vision-rapt in whirl of song cried out"	156
78 When Rumi vision-rapt in whirl of song cried out	**157**
Thoughts on "A lyric diary will map the road"	158
79 A lyric diary will map the road	**159**
Thoughts on "Repent is linked to pain, regret to weep"	160
80 *Repent* is linked to pain, *regret* to weep	**161**
Thoughts on "The diabetic takes a daily test"	162
81 The diabetic takes a daily test	**163**
Thoughts on "I feel the urge to sing, but—what of this?"	164
82 I feel the urge to sing, but—what of this?	**165**
Thoughts on "Depict the moments from within: you'll know them more"	166
83 Depict the moments from within: you'll know them more	**167**
Thoughts on "A part of what enabled me to sing"	168
84 A part of what enabled me to sing	**169**
Thoughts on "What Swinburne called a nympholept am I"	170
85 What Swinburne called a nympholept am I	**171**

Thoughts on "To seek the most arousing way to read"   *172*
   86 To seek the most arousing way to read   **173**

Thoughts on "Came the rehearsal break, I heard the festive bell"   *174*
   87 Came the rehearsal break, I heard the festive bell   **175**

Thoughts on "Inhabiting the lines you're acting out"   *176*
   88 Inhabiting the lines you're acting out   **177**

Thoughts on "A program lacking thesis or a plan"   *178*
   89 A program lacking thesis or a plan   **179**

Thoughts on "Each hint you in the shine of eyes can see"   *180*
   90 Each hint you in the shine of eye can see   **181**

Thoughts on "The wonder wasn't quite bewilderment"   *182*
   91 The wonder wasn't quite bewilderment   **183**

Thoughts on "The night of quietude, my friend"   *184*
   92 The night of quietude, my friend   **185**

Thoughts on "Unconscious cowing by authorities"   *186*
   93 Unconscious cowing by authorities   **187**

Thoughts on "Said Enterpriser to the Undertaker"   *188*
   94 Said Enterpriser to the Undertaker   **189**

Thoughts on "Let's overtake the poet world by storm"   *190*
   95 Let's overtake the poet world by storm   **191**

Thoughts on "The hero and the minstrel may unite"   *192*
   96 The hero and the minstrel may unite   **193**

Thoughts on "I join the fingertips of left and right"   *194*
   97 I join the fingertips of left and right   **195**

Thoughts on "Place all your expectations where you will"   *196*

98 Place all your expectations where you will 197

Thoughts on "Fall trees, pure red, rich orange, come to seem"   *198*

99 Fall trees, pure red, rich orange, come to seem   **199**

Thoughts on "Cease not imagining what yet can be"   *200*

100 Cease not imagining what yet can be   **201**

Name Index   **203**

INTRODUCTION

Villanelles are fun to write and to read—no wonder they're popular. You may be familiar with one or more of these: "Do not go gentle into that good night" by Dylan Thomas, "The Waking" ("I wake to sleep, and take my waking slow") by Theodore Roethke, and "One Art" ("The art of losing isn't hard to master") by Elizabeth Bishop.

Oddly, most writers who've done villanelles appear to have written very few of them. A book of a hundred is not common. And a hundred villanelles with blogatelles? You're holding what may be the first one yet attempted.

What is a villanelle? A short poem with a couple of strategically placed recurrent lines or "refrains" that lend the music a rural quality—the French word *villein* referred to farmers. And a blogatelle? I invented this word to mean a cross between a blog and a "bagatelle," a French-derived term meaning simply a light musical piece. "Bagatelles" were pioneered (in suites of them) by Beethoven, who in a way typical of him deepened their value beyond all previous imagining. Béla Bartók's bagatelles are wonderful, too, with Eastern European ethnic flavors. Originally the word meant little more than a toss-off, a trifle, and Beethoven called some of his earlier bagatelles *Kleinigkeiten*, "little things." So my blogatelles are meant to be conversational and casual. That they might acquire a measure of depth while unfolding in colloquy with the adjoining poems would be a wonderful thing to hope. The idea of a blogatelle came to me when I realized that I was trying to create in this format a kind of flowing, musical prose that would go well with the poetry.

My villanelles and blogatelle comments are filled with references to religious and mythic legacies—Christian, Islamic, Jewish, Greco-Roman and other—and I've provided a Name Index of the people and writings I mention. But the poet who speaks (or rather, sings) in this book never plays the role of a believer. He's an imaginer—not a lowly mode of thought and action but an emulation of the highest (see *God the All-Imaginer: Wisdom of Sufi Master Ibn Arabi in 99 Modern Sonnets* in the bibliography at the end). My only religion is gratitude for breathing while my heart is inhaling the sky. The enlivened air begins to sing in me, and I create to mirror the Creation. The villanelles in this book are hymns to both kinds of creativity, the one that powers the pluriverse and the one that flowers in journey-verse.

Because I only became a musical lyric translator at age 59, a writer of original verse at 61, I'm attracted to the Sufi practice of alertness to the Name that "calls" you to your "vocation" (see comments on poems 4, 5, 7). The 99 names of God in the Qur'an may be read as potentials of Becoming that you can freely adopt when summoned by one of them that specially attracts you. My thoughts on poems 6 and 7 end with Qur'an quotations: I'd like for these to become as common in "western" writing as Bible phrases have often been. I travel around, though, in the world of scriptures: poem 9 is based on the Buddhist-influenced Hindu *Bhagavad-Gita*. And I apply the speculative thoughts to object-events of my daily life: rocking-chair (#8, #48, #49), cat (#9), coffee (#27), thunder (#10).

Poem 11 acknowledges the Unmanifest in both the individual human and the cosmic Source. We don't really know ourselves, despite what the oracle advised Socrates in ancient times, and although God has 99 Names in the Qur'an, these are merely attributes or qualities of something whose deep, essential Being is forever unknown, unattainable. Everything we see or feel, hear or touch around us can only be a metaphor of the Unmanifest beyond the reach of finite mortals. What an opening for poets—whose labor of love is the making of metaphor!

All faiths, creeds, beliefs, and religions are containers for the water of spirit—a Sufi teaching that I love (central to #41 and #44). In poem 12 I point out the resemblance of two images: the eye of ancient Egyptian god Horus and the eye on the palm of the hand shown on the modern Middle Eastern ḥamsa, a good luck charm found as readily in Israel as in Egypt, to name two places I have toured. In poem 13 each of us, with our unmanifest depth, is a metaphor, a symbol or parable-emblem, tossed up by the Ocean of the Greater Unmanifest. Surrealist artists and poets, with their love for the randomly "found object" as a stimulator of the imagination, are at one with many major thinkers in their alertness to metaphoric possibilities hiding in everything: Newton's pebble on the sea shore, Wordsworth's cloud-gap through which the lower-lying ocean could suddenly be heard, Goethe's belief that "occasion"—happening, random chance—was the key to everything he wrote, and finally (if I may include this) my own finding that rhymes are revelators of seemingly unrelated connections.

Unsuspected connections may show seeming contraries are really points along a unified continuum. In Poem 14 I recommend being open to the metaphoric powers of spectrum-sexuality. As the spectrum of light offers rainbow diversity contained in a oneness, the immense variability of human sexuality has broad metaphoric value. Bisexual Shakespeare learned this when he wrote 154 sonnets addressed to boyfriend and girlfriend. Most human languages illustrate the same exploratory openness by assigning gender to nearly everything. My own experience taught me this when I came to realize that a poet, novelist, or playwright needs the ability to imagine every kind of sexuality in order to create realistic human characters with the vast metaphoric range of potentials that people really have. Poem 25 culminates the spectrum theme: here I recommend considering nearly every sort of human behavior as placeable on a spectrum, a continuum, a continuity that avoids inaccurately conceived good-vs.-bad or me-vs.-you disjunctions and conflicts.

In Poem 15 I invoke the teaching of Sufi master Ibn Arabi that Essential Being will disclose itself obliquely, indirectly, only in rapid glimpses, and never the same way twice. To perceive the metaphoric potentials in your own life, you need extreme alertness: metaphoric possibility (epiphany, relevation, the Aha! moment) may be mixed thoroughly with what seems mundane and everyday. In Poem 16 I advocate extending the spectrum concept from #14 to help us deal with just about everything we encounter. Bipolarism, for example, often shows the two "poles" blended, the high and the low combined in manic agitation or in our wild recklessness when feeling abandoned. The smile of Buddha and the tear of Jesus meld in many of our moments (#17).

The next few poems, despite their acknowledgment of problems, point to reasons for gratitude in daily life. In poem 18 I give thanks for both science and art, largely to defend the former from its backward-looking present-day detractors, the wealthy few. In #19 I give thanks for daily freedom, earned after teaching for 35 years, to tend my garden of assiduously planted verse. Returning to applied science, in poem 20 I give thanks for the cheap and simple electric fan that powers my environment for a livable summer (no air conditioning in my house: the trees are good enough, the gentle maples and the lordly weeping willow). Poem 21 tells of staying mindful to the musical or sculptural potency of each passing moment when alertly focused on and versed.

The alertness theme leads to the idea in #22 that as we make art out of observed and pondered moments we can invent values and even (it isn't too much say of the best of poets) become a living scripture. Indeed, the Dylan Thomas villanelle I cite in the opening of this Intro ("Do not go gentle into that good night") is quoted by many with as much admiration as the Bible or Shakespeare—and I, too, fondly recall him in #23.

Next we have a group of lyrics illustrating ways to affirm life. Molten glass and lasting "dead" bouquet recall to me again the peace in Being taught by my late father, a student of Spinoza (#26). Speeding up my heart for love-labor, coffee gets me going on my challenging task: to be a singer who's the Homer of his own odyssey (#27 and blogatelle, also #73). Poet William Blake sang right up to the last moment of his life—not "raging" like the speaker in Thomas' villanelle, but *praising* (#28). Poems 29 and 30 belong together. The first one shows how little we know either of ourselves or of the beyond—and yet the Unmanifest that is a part of both may harbor godly potential. In the second poem, another threatening negativity is overcome by its positive counteraction: a crisis in my life opened the unknown treasure that was hiding for 59 years till forced into my awareness.

Poems 31–35 are a rounded group of lighter verses enfolded in the more ambitious bookend poems—about a summons or vocation (a "calling") from the Unmanifest—that begin and end the section. In #31 I return to the theme of poems 11 and 29: the Unmanifest in both you and the beyond, a darkness out of which appears a potential hitherto hidden (in you, or in the beyond), an unsuspected disclosure that summons you now by the Name that may become your own. (Later, in #45 and #46, the "summoner" becomes the overarching theme. In the latter I compare him to the three angels who were the guests of Abraham in the Bible.) In #35 I develop the summoning-theme by unfolding the Sufi teaching (of Ibn Arabi) that night is emphatically no mere void: it is, in dark and in silence, the provider of two metaphors for the Unmanifest, which contains both death and unsuspected life. In between these two bracketing lyrics, I offer playful applications of the main idea: Explore your potential. The unifying mood of all three is Fun. Poem 32 advocates teaching little kids to recite and write villanelles. (Why not? Give me three good reasons.) Poem 33 equates poem-writing events to sport events: both are exciting, take work, and thoroughly satisfy. Poem 34 and the blogatelle comment play around with word shapes. Later in #42 I even tell about writing for children, and in #43 the spirit of word*play* is active.

We go on to explore a few intriguing paradoxes. In #36 we find that the very word "identity" is a paradox: the Latin root *idem* means "same," but our identities are—especially if we encourage them to be so—continually changing as we acquire new "names." Poem 37 shows the paradox of anger: it kills the angry, not the so-called offender, who may in any case not really be guilty (think of the "spectrum" idea in poem 25: human behavior in nearly every activity or situation is placeable in a continuum—good-vs.-evil categories are most often useless). Poem 38 gave me a chance for a self-directed sermonette. Having been a "teacher" for 35 years, I talked a lot, and when you do that you might forget the distortions inherent in speaking—in talk of any kind. There's a paradox in the fact that a clearly structured sentence gives what might look like a clear structure to things that are mostly unclear to us.

The paradox in the 39th villanelle broadens in the blogatelle. Yes, the underworld of mind is ocean-wide, defying the limits both of space and time, but the waking world of the physical heavens at night is equally important if you're interested in destroying a falsely constraining view of yourself. The history of the universe is portrayed up there: the light you're getting this minute from any given star was emitted at a different time from the lights of other stars, and all come from what is almost unimaginably old. What happened back then is what you're seeing this minute—it took that long to get to you.

I feel a bit dizzy thinking of this, and when that happens I write such a poem as #40, recalling the Sufi teaching that we are dreamers who are dreamed. You can look at this idea mystically (God is dreaming us) or psychologically (the Unconscious is dreaming the fears and desires that will motivate and shape the "us" of daytime action). I feel at all times like a dreamer when I'm writing, very much at sea "upon a sea of Seem." That accounts for what you hear in #47, where I'm as eager to apply astrology and horoscopy to my imaginative task as to use the scriptures and myths of any of the world's religions. I would always rather be an imaginer than a believer.

In poems 49 and 50 and in the blogatelles to #46 and #48, I develop the theme of the literary "epiphany," the revelation that may as readily be called secular as sacred, that a poet (or novelist, or playwright, or mathematician—Henri Poincaré has written of his own and other mathematicians' visual epiphanies!) may have at any time. These are the same, I think, as the "disclosures" whereby the Unknowable and Unnamable is given opaque and partial yet still revelatory reality to the seer, prophet, artist, poet. In *Patterns of Epiphany,* with the help of theorist Gaston Bachelard, I trace recurrent patterns of element-movement-shape in some of the greatest imaginers we have. In the four places mentioned above I describe the signature epiphanies of Elizabeth Barrett Browning, Charlotte Brontë, Thomas Carlyle, S. T. Coleridge, Walter Pater, and Alfred, Lord

Tennyson. In *God the All-Imaginer* there's a bibliography of other studies I've done in this field and the book itself contains a study of the epiphanies of Ibn Arabi.

I've observed that in today's world, with no traditional moorings for a writer in aristocratic patronage, authors have to make their own way, and that means you'll need to be sailor and minstrel both—the journeyer and the journaler, the Odysseus who makes an odyssey and the Homer who writes it up (see vii above, poem 73, and the blogatelles to #27, #45, #52). In poems 51–53 I focus on the attitude of the writer playing this double role. Poem 51 shows humor lessening the tensions of rivalry with other authors (humor's a favorite topic of mine and keeps coming back: see #42 and #71). In poem 52 we learn, as all the epic heroes that made the deep descent had learned, how to fall and rise again. In #53 I remember, as I must continue to do, that we're all dreamers, we're possibly even dreams (cf. #40). Poem 55 shows how to maintain the spirit that motivates the perseverance I mention in #54: just keep in mind that for walkers on the spherical earth all skyward directions are up.

Motion is my focus in the next couple of poems: #56 tells of my mentor, medieval Persian poet Rumi, founder of the Whirling Dervishes, who "heavened hell" in his revolutionary teaching that all Creation is one great fire circling around God, and that we are each a flaming atomic energy-particle moving in that circling dance. I move the motion-theme forward in #57 by suggesting that if we really want a "liberal"—liber*ating*—education, we need to travel throughout cultural and physical space and time, to become a part of things. In #61 I return to the theme of motion, suggesting that even the words "random" and "chance" grow from word-roots meaning "run" and "fall."

In #58 I extend my earlier "summoner" or "guest" theme (#45, #46) by declaring myself a member of what a well-known movie called the "Dead Poets Society." In fact, most of my mentors in the craft of writing do turn out to be "dead": few living people I've met love word music as much as I do. In #59 I wonder how people with mentalities like mine are surviving nowadays. In #60 I suggest that whenever Shakespeare's verbal music is left unheard in a performance and only the dramatic action comes through, as a word musician the "immortal" poet dies and dies again. In #62 my own death will mean that the unity of body and spirit will morph into the unity of the vanished friend and the one who remains alive. In #63, however, I look at the word "sublime" and find that, rootwise, it meant "go the limit"! Science gives me unheard of chances to continue living—but only if I push against the limits in a way that stays productive. Productivity, I show in #64, is opposed to hoarding. It means loving generosity—the central active virtue in all the religious traditions I can find. And in #65 I discover generosity in what seemed an unlikely place: I've found it in the weakening of recent memory as I get older. When I turn to poems recently composed and already forgotten, they seem written by someone else—and if they're attractive, I'm surprised how much I want to thank "him" for doing me the favor!

From the theme of generosity we pass readily to the next thematic focus: friendship. Poem 66 puts it plainly: the difference between a psychosis and a poem is a friend. In #67 I write of a friend of mine who has been an irreplaceable helper to many, having quit his academic post in musicology to minister full-time to the dying in a hospice. In the following poems I explore in a lighter vein the ways the poem you are writing can be itself a friend to you. The pleasures of a varied syntax delight the maker-mind in #68. The click of computer keys can bring back a memory of organ recitals in #69. And the white of the computer screen—color of encompassing and of endless potential—recalls the Prophet Muhammad's comparison of knowledge to milk, as I show in #70. Poem 72 explores the poet's function as a friend to others. Poem 74 reintroduces the olden theme of the poet's friend as mentor-muse, goddess of inspiration, in the form of Queen Mab or Irish Maeve.

Though present-day political dilemmas get me down in #71 and #75, I have what I call "happy brain chemicals"— I'm not skilled at dwelling on regrettable situations to be (or maybe never to be) remedied. So typically, for better or for worse (and of course for me the "better" will seem more prominent), I seek relief with humor or playfulness, a mood I lovingly cultivate. Whimsically presented, if seriously meant, is the proposal in #76 for National Iambic Pentameter Day, and in #77 I enjoy watching a German shepherd attempt to "shepherd" the waves in a San Francisco bay. In #78 I explain that for my favorite mystic poet Rumi the other half of "affliction" is always "yes," and he makes a pun about it. In #79 and its blogatelle I offer a foursome of trusty key words for a tempered optimism. A handy Buddhist therapy technique to get rid of remorse and regret will be found in poem 80.

Then I switch to "phenomenology of daily life"— brief treatments of everyday insights or problems that arise, at times occasioning little sermonette villanelles. In #81 I consider diabetic discipline; in #82 I deal with unreasoned fears of weekly computer updates. In #83 I turn to objective study, practicing "phenomenological bracketing"—close observation of what's happening to me—by concentrating on how the body feels when smiling. A comparable experiment is performed later in #97 as I compare the left- and right-minded sensations of two hands touching in the Dürer prayer position. Two more brief self-scrutinies: what it feels like to write in a steady beat (#84) and what it feels like to have an ecstatic "fit" (#85).

Five poems next allow me to wander among memories of letting other poets mentor me. In #86 thoughts on rhythm lead me to George Gordon, Lord Byron and (in the blogatelle) to the powerful meters in the songs of James Macpherson's faked compositions of an ancient Scot, Ossian. In #87 I remember Goethe's poems about Mejnoun and Laila, the Romeo and Juliet of the Middle East. In Poems 88 and 89 I get to re-live my YouTube presentation, together with Marina Zalesski, of Russia's world-traveler poet Nikolay Gumilev. If you want to look at the YouTube (a nice hour-and-a-half entertainment, which has had over 600 viewers) you'll get an even better idea of what that theater-piece felt like to create and to experience. Poem 90 grows out of this, too, as I reflect on the way a spark in the eye of student, friend, or colleague moves my imagination to new thoughts about the poetry we're considering.

All the rest of the lyrics that follow could be called an extended pep talk, as we move from #91 on the guidance of a mentor-friend, to #92 on the night as perfect work-time, to #93 on removing the residues of paternalism in life and mind, to #94 on mentors in Romantic poetry (Goethe, Wordsworth, Byron), until finally in #95 we're ready to take the poet world by storm, coordinating the two mental horses of Plato and then riding on the heaven-directed steed of Muhammad. To cap the climax of the theme, in #96 and blogatelle, Bellerophon joins us on yet another flying horse while we note the origin of all such visionary travel in the world-wide culture of the shaman, whose drum is turned into his skiey charger—document and vehicle the same, the minstrel and the hero joined in one, a person-performance. Poem 98 sums up multi-stage rhapsode-therapy in the motto, "Place all your expectations where you will, / And self-declared requirement then fulfill." The book's concluding hymns can celebrate the autumn of life with the prior poems' encouragements kept hearteningly in mind.

A Hundred VILLANELLES

A Hundred BLOGATELLES

Thoughts on "A slender veil, a tender trance"

The "muse," Greek name for an art-inspiring goddess, blends with the "houri," a female spirit in Islamic heaven. Speaker and Lady Inspirer are two in one, the writer and his secret heart or deeper dream-thought. Rising from the Unconscious, she remains in part obscured.

The symmetry of our body intimates a balanced two-sidedness. The rhythmic dance of the poem to be written unifies author and houri-muse—a dance of adameve, in praise of the greater unity that subsumes them, that created them.

She tells him of a love that transcends the sad by including it in the One. The first chapter of the Qur'an, called "The Opening," is said in the morning when the poet is prostrate in devotion, as are the grasses before the oversweeping wind.

In prayer we may be called by one of God's 99 Names given in the Qur'an. Yes, we call on God's Name, but a Name can equally summon us—to fulfil the potentials it emblemizes, potencies that want to become actualities by attaining existence in the Worlds. If we identify with a Name and embody it, God Himself attains greater fullness of being, and as for us, we find out who we are. Such is the teaching of Ibn Arabi, chief of the Sufi masters.

Dew is like tears, a beam of light can pierce vision as a lance might do: pain and pleasure, striving and reward, are One. The Lady is veiled and entranced, and so too the beholder who knows her with the half-disclosed knowledge that is metaphor. We ascend through likenesses: our essential Being and Lords remain unknown.

1 A slender veil, a tender trance

A slender veil, a tender trance:
My houri muse I here may view
Dark-eyed reply in twilit glance.

Await a loved and shunned romance:
The One must play a game of two—
A slender veil, a tender trance.

The body's even atom-dance
Has adameve as hallelu:
Dark-eyed reply in twilit glance.

Can sad the happy man enhance?
Long-shadowed prostrate lawn, 'tis you:
A slender veil, a tender trance.

Abscondent in our happenstance
We're nameless all till name be new,
Dark-eyed reply in twilit glance.

An angel tear, a sunbeam lance,
A hope, a fear—deep dole adieu!
A slender veil, a tender trance,
Dark-eyed reply in twilit glance.

Thoughts on "The planet on creation day"

In the Jewish prayer book, there's a line I can't forget: "He renews every day the work of creation." I elaborate that theme. The existence of the world on any random day is fully as great a marvel as occurred on its day of origin. What you're looking at might just as well have been made a moment ago, for it is in the process of being remade every nanosecond.

Second tercet: every breath is a world-starter.

Third tercet: the bird that sings to a sun not yet risen brings to mind a prophet who can foresee what's yet unknown.

Fourth tercet: the miracle of the low is no less than that of the high. Worm castings fertilize the earth and make possible the crops that feed us. Charles Darwin realized that without the worms we'd have no farm. Rightly may we bow our heads in reverence and look straight downward.

The willow wands on my giant backyard tree that sweep the earth in tender strokes are acting out their lovesong to the source of what is high and low.

The Tao (pronounced "Dow") of Chinese mystic thought is a hidden Way, the Law of "Let it be," which today brings back the day of origin, for it exerted quiet power then as now. Here's William Blake in his "Auguries of Innocence": "If the Sun and Moon should doubt, / They'd immediately go out." Every form of being is an act of faith or confidence, whether conscious or not.

2 The planet on creation day

The planet on creation day
From nothing came. 'Tis making now
What vainly doubter might gainsay.

Inhaling breath, let not dismay
The Hand that Being would allow
The planet on creation day.

A bird traversing higher way
Avers to earth, we ken not how,
What vainly doubter might gainsay.

The worms that fertilize the clay—
To them would recommend we bow
The planet on creation day.

The willow boughs that supple sway
Caress the ground and thus endow
What vainly doubter might gainsay.

The Tao in each, the sage will say,
Can not impeach, nor disavow,
The planet on creation day—
What vainly doubter might gainsay.

Thoughts on "A cinch, a snap, when we've a knack"

Tremendous fun—wouldn't kids in school love to try a villanelle? Gods eat ambrosia and drink nectar: neither is more pleasant than a tricky, appealing craft well-mastered.

Happiness in a perfected skill gives you energy to keep enjoying it through more and more varied productivity in that form. "Limber" is a favorite word of mine, meaning "relaxed in being well-practiced." It brings to mind other word treasures: "lithe," "limpid," "fluid," flight." Any animal well exercised and at ease in its own body invigorates the human eye.

Confidence that leaps to the heart through skill turns every lack to luck. A church bell heard seems to greet life, not to commemorate death.

The last two sections of the poem vary the theme of practice as itself perfection: the harder I work, the luckier I get. Looking at both craftsmanship and life as a journey toward growing insight, we gain added energy for the task and joy. The pilgrim, positing a distant goal, takes pleasure in each of the journey's innumerable stages.

Skill and impulse are at one in *sprezzatura,* the art concealing art. Traces of all effort hide, for the act seems effortless. The nightingale is our example in the singing world. It has at least half a dozen songs to choose from. Yes, there will be repetition, but given so much variety, the welcomed familiarities accentuate the diversity. It happens with villanelles.

3 A cinch, a snap, when we've a knack

A cinch, a snap, when we've a knack
For lyric is a villanelle.
Skill, impulse pay the favor back.

Ambrosial, nectar-sweet, a snack
That, tasteful, of the gods may tell:
A cinch, a snap, when we've a knack.

Adrift, with grace of wind, on track,
With limber syntax rhyming well,
Skill, impulse pay the favor back.

A liking turns to luck a lack
With morning chime in knolling bell:
A cinch, a snap, when we've a knack.

Bring pilgrim staff and travel sack
And sandal shoon 'mid sand-dune swell:
Skill, impulse pay the favor back.

The maker takes another tack
When first he fails—a better spell:
A cinch, a snap, when we've a knack:
Skill, impulse pay the favor back.

Thoughts on "Form is the way we hold our art"

My friend poet-playright Grace Cavalieri made the initial statement that triggered this poem.

The second tercet embodies a thought of Ibn Arabi, major interpreter of mystical Sufism. He says every religion, creed, doctrine, or god is a cup that gives form and color to the water of spirit.

Tercet three draws on a Spanish folk song: *Cantar que sube alla boca / es una gota de miel / que del corazon reboza.* Song that to the lips will come / Is a drop of honey which / Overflows the brimming heart.

Tidal movement aids our song or chant by making us mindful of our own steady heartbeat. Hearing meter echoed in the skies may have motivated thinkers of the Pythagorean school to guess that the ratios between the distances of the planets from earth may correlate to the ratios between the intervals that need to be marked off by the finger on a fiddle-string to cause the harmony to arise.

The sweetness of a piercing love may overpower the helmsman of our spirit-craft, yet when moderated in the measured rhythm of narrative ballads it might not torment but tease.

The tides of the salty ocean encompass and enfold, transcend while sounding in their cosmic power the tears of love, which is our breath of life.

4 Form is the way we hold our art

Form is the way we hold our art,
A poet said. Aroma breeze
I breathe, and body so impart.

The wine, the water are the start
And end as well, but cup will please:
Form is the way we hold our art.

If honeydrop the brimming heart
Should overflow, we'll sing with ease:
I breathe, and body so impart.

We ocean sail with starry chart:
The motion aids our melodies.
Form is the way we hold our art.

When angel arrow, eros dart
Distract, in ballad let them tease.
I breathe, and body so impart.

The tides, that can the tears outsmart,
Have smiled on all the changing me's.
Form is the way we hold our art.
I breathe, and body so impart.

Thoughts on "Computer update—change at hand"

I'm not a "handy" guy and don't like the idea of learning a new machine each week. But the new Word program policy of hebdomadal updates needn't have scared me: their improvements have made writing easier.

"Overmind" is a word in memory of Ralph Waldo Emerson's "Oversoul." I use it when I'm seeing things predestined to help me move in a new direction.

Retirement from college teaching thirteen years ago was the biggest chance for a life-changing path: instead of interpreting the works of poets the way I'd done for 35 years, I now had a chance to become a verse writer. It changed my name: Jacob became Israel.

Making my life into verbal music added a depth-height to my wandering. The pilgrim's made spelunker, aviator, for the unconscious lifts you high when you take the plunge. Freedom emerges when you discover what you didn't know you had in you. So in the final quatrain I tell my inner light to shine in cave or cloud.

In mystical Sufi speculation, the 99 Attributes of God are embodied in angels who summon people by speaking their own names. The angel-name refers to a potential in God's mind that you personally may be suited to develop on earth and so to enrich His Being. If you identify with the prospect held out to you, that godly name becomes your own. You won't be the person you were before.

5 Computer update—change at hand

Computer update—change at hand:
Though much delay might irritate,
Await a kindlier command.

The overmind, you'll understand,
Has undermined things stale of late:
Computer update—change at hand.

Withdraw, resile. Contract, expand
The mind: receive a high estate:
Await a kindlier command.

One maps upon a plane what's planned.
Who'll depth-dimension calculate?
Computer update—change at hand.

To take account might countermand
Weak freedom dealing with our fate:
Await a kindlier command.

Not contraband, but comrade-band.
Let, light, the past evaporate,
Computer update—change at hand.
Await a kindlier command.

Thoughts on "To the extent that love allows"

The third line could be translated like this: "Freed from the past, we direct our planning to the future." In my teenage years I liked the love songs of e. e. cummings (can you tell?).

Cloudy-browed Jove is merely bad weather. The Romans called gloomy sky "malus Iuppiter," an ill-disposed god-king. Thunderstorms are worth the lilies they nourish, whose glory I relate to Solomon's: he finds their noble beauty akin to his own high estate, a mood that Jesus entered by his lily parable.

The final tercet needs a bit of syntactical agility to be read in the best way: it is a hidden wit, secret wisdom, that is endowing the water-dowser with a gift when he detects rivers underground, as they are depicted in Islamic Eden. I love this emblem of unconscious life and vital strength.

Don't sleep too late, you'll miss the resurrection day. Continuing the playful mood begun with cummings, in these words I'm offering a riddle. The Qur'an holds the answer. "25:47. And it is he who maketh night a covering for you, and sleep repose, and maketh day a resurrection."

6 To the extent that love allows

To the extent that love allows
No dismal mist need mood dismay:
Un-from'd we to-ify our hows.

Joy-roisterer will ray arouse—
Though januarial be May—
To the extent that love allows.

On lilies then we graze or browse
Entranced in Solomonic way:
Un-from'd we to-ify our hows.

Forgive great Jove his cloudy brows
That olden petulance betray—
To the extent that love allows.

The dowser hidden wit endows
Where underground the waters play:
Un-from'd we to-ify our hows.

Let not too long the spirit drowse—
You'll miss the resurrection day:
To the extent that love allows
Un-from'd we to-ify our hows.

Thoughts on "An avian poet sings at four"

Four is the bird hour: the prophet-creatures prepare to herald the sun they don't yet see. The wind feels like a force opening a door: Latin *limen* means threshold: a threshold moment for the spirit is "liminal." Latin *lumen* means light, and it's revealing that threshold and light should sound so alike in that beautiful language. When the door of a home is opened, light spreads out over the threshold.

Your "soul-name" is what I called your "angel name" in the thoughts on "5. Computer Update": this spiritual name sums up the particular Divine potential that you are called to embody if you want, a name that, if you identify with it, will become your own so long as you wish.

Bird calls have, for me, a cooling sound, like the visible effect of silver. The name that calls you (a lovable paradox) can be an expression emphasizing either Life or Knowledge, the two Trees singled out in Eden. The trees in the Bible account are contrasted, but I equate them at the root.

Bird calls are so amazingly vehement, coming with relentless strength and volume from tiny beings, that I think of them as friendly poetic or athletic rivals of the coming sunlight in prophetic power.

At 4 AM I silent wait for the dawn the birds predict. The light will shortly begem the dew, whose appearance all living beings feel to be a mercy. In Qur'an 21:107 God declares He sent the Prophet "as a mercy to the worlds."

7 An avian poet sings at four

An avian poet sings at four.
The phrase for heaven's sake will stay:
The wind becomes an open door.

New soul-name you'll in tunes outpour
Whose rhythm brings a later ray:
An avian poet sings at four.

They're borne away to golden shore
Who tones more cold than silver play:
The wind becomes an open door.

A Tree desire can be the core:
The seed a Let It Be will say.
An avian poet sings at four.

The choiring light with sun may war,
Nor cede the gain to lucent day.
The wind becomes an open door.

Let liminal be lumen for
The dawn the dew on lawn will lay.
An avian poet sings at four.
The wind becomes an open door.

Thoughts on "How place-like our container, Time"

Hebrew *olam,* like Arabic *alam,* refers at once to two things that are unbounded: space and time. Keeping the two in mind at once may help you feel headed somewhere and yet always at the central heart.

Seasons hint at a cycle, but the pattern they provide cannot satisfy entirely. Therefore Rudolf Steiner made a spiral the emblem of his theosophic thought. We can move upward and enlarge our circumference in the height dimension.

Another meeting place of central yet directional energy in space and time is rhythmed verse, echoing the heartbeat. Meditation in a rocking-chair can relate you to the ocean tides. A rocking-chair is a place that keeps time.

Up-and-down, back-and-forth may suggest the strong-and-weak rhythm structures in every line of metric (metered = rhythmed) poetry. Rhymes, too, are the same returning with a difference.

There's a coziness to place that may appear absent from flowing time. I'm protected from the terrors of audible nothingness by the whisper-like sound in my ears. I can wait in my chair at the keyboard till a word music arrives. But time is newness every minute: each heartbeat is a resurrection.

Deep breathing keeps you in motion wherever you are.

8 How place-like our container, Time

How place-like our container, Time:
Becoming's cradled, safe, ensured.
We tidal-swayed breathe life in rhyme.

While, craving breadth or height to climb,
By stream, steed, plane one feels allured,
How place-like our container, Time.

Impatient with primeval slime,
Though rise a slow inertia cured,
We tidal-swayed breathe life in rhyme.

How swift soever in their prime,
Folk may in speed-pride stay immured.
How place-like our container, Time.

Reshaping of a paradigm
Can make the heart to care inured:
We tidal-swayed breathe life in rhyme.

Upheld in palm of space-friend I'm
Content, false worry long abjured.
How place-like our container, Time:
We tidal-swayed breathe life in rhyme.

Thoughts on "The giant cat will govern fate"

What brought all this on was a digital photo of a Russian cat belonging to an extra-large breed, delightful to see, and recalling varieties called Norwegian Forest Cat and Maine Coon Cat.

He resembles all other cats I've known in seeming to have two types or levels of awareness. Cats are efficient predators—too effective, perhaps: they kill more creatures than they want to eat. But when asleep and apurr, or even if awake and gently relaxed, they appear to have attained nirvana or satori. They bring to mind the Buddhist-influenced Hindu scripture called *Bhagavad-Gita,* where the warrior Árjuna, weary of unending battle, is counseled by Vishnu, embodied in the human form of Krishna, that one should fight, if this be a social obligation, with a distanced mind, a mentality centered on higher things that matter (things beyond mere matter). So a cat can switch from meditative to predatory mode, rapidly back and forth.

In meditation we feel that Brahma(n) the Creator and Atman the individual soul are inseparable and coessential (sharing the same state and mode of Being). Cat and cosmos are one.

I can't help remembering the first revelatory cat I saw in art: a cat depicted by a professional animal painter who had developed schizophrenia. My late mother, a physician, would receive a monthly free magazine called *MD* with articles on humanistic culture for medically trained readers. The feline was envisioned in a form of a six-winged seraph or fiery angel, with pensive cat-calm face.

9 The giant cat will govern fate

The giant cat will govern fate:
For changing hour, an altered mind—
A spirit key: to meditate.

Gray, tan, black, white, by winter wait
In Russia he is unconfined:
The giant cat will govern fate.

He's tranquil. Energies abate.
A spring's for hunting been designed.
A spirit key: to meditate.

Wild strength can with the season mate
To which predations are assigned.
The giant cat will govern fate.

Hears Árjuna god Krishna state:
Fight when you must, yet be not blind.
A spirit key: to meditate.

An act that some parade as great
Think distant. Brahman-Atman's kind.
The giant cat will govern fate.
A spirit key: to meditate.

Thoughts on "The thunder beauty first may shock"

Line one is a riddle. Does it mean "The beauty of thunder may at first prove shocking"? or "The thunder may at first prove shocking to beauty"?

Naturally the answer is "Yes." Because so many of our feelings are mixed, literary art conveys the conflict with double-valued phrasing. Formerly a teacher of literary studies, I'll tell you a trick I often used to make this point. Typically questions in class would follow a paradigm: "This passage might have meaning A, and it might have meaning B. Is A correct or is B correct?" I'd answer, "Yes."

Norwegian deities Thor and Freya, Storm and Passion (who gave their names to Thursday and Friday), let loose what will shock and, equally, impress. A dog may run to hide in his sheltering box. A person who's upset may become more so.

But thunder is only our heartbeat amplified, as drum playing in rituals around the world speaks of the gods. Our life shouldn't ever seem as stable as a rock, but as volatile as the heaven. In fact, even a rock, to a world-class microscope, is a whirlwind of energy-particles, particulate energies that never stop.

The heartbeat gets louder, pounds harder in passion. And everything beautiful arouses passion, mild or extreme, predictable or wildly strange. First we are shocked out of our beautiful comfort by thunder, then shocked to find how much more alive we are when becoming thunderous.

10 The thunder beauty first may shock

The thunder beauty first may shock.
Our frightened dogs will patient hide.
Our habit-mind it must unblock.

Thor, Freya, love and war, unlock
Their kindred forces that collide:
The thunder beauty first may shock.

A surge in urgency will mock
What lazy wiles had long let slide:
Our habit-mind it must unblock.

Comes water forth from drums that talk,
Then shout, *Wise-active gods abide!*
The thunder beauty first may shock.

There's naught more solid than the rock,
Yet rocking sky can lightning guide!
Our habit-mind it must unblock.

The sheepish fear to leave their flock,
But eagle wills are purified.
The thunder beauty first may shock:
Our habit-mind it must unblock.

Thoughts on "The quiet which at night will come"

Sufi thinker Ibn Arabi taught me this about night: it is not an experience of the void, or nullity or nihilation. Darkness is not nothing, far from it. We view it as a palpable thing that is there. Not a time of fear, but of solace, even joy in the fact that, instead of nil, we see a new and renewing entity, a state of being, and one we may gratefully share.

Night may emblemize death in its darkness but life in its depth. And therefore it stimulates life. In one of my best-loved excerpts, we learn what's crucial here from the Qur'an: "73:5. For we [Allah, the "imperial we"] shall charge thee with a word of weight. 6. Lo! the vigil of the night is (a time) when impression is more keen and speech more certain."

Night is "the nothing and the sum" viewed in sequence. We note a huge disappearance. But then the spirit feels the deep, which calls to the deep in us. Night is like the Unmanifest in ourselves and in the Creative Source. For both self and Source the visible is the metaphoric likeness, not the essential Being. From an unknown depth we issue forth, and the knowledge of that emerging is an encompassing completeness, an absorbing contemplation from which awareness will at times awake as the thinking that masters the deep when imagining surrenders to the greater One, making room for it in the partly-fathomed heart.

From this point of view and of feeling, the point of light where thought joins the Unthinkable, can Wisdom arise, the Indwelling Presence (an insight I learned from Steinsaltz' edition of Zalman's *Tanya*). White contains the spectrum of colors. Night contains the spectrum of metaphors yet to emerge.

11 The quiet which at night will come

The quiet which at night will come
Means doubly much. 'Twill softly hold
The depth it is emerging from.

It is the nothing and the sum,
A mercy to the thoughtful-souled,
The quiet which at night will come.

'Twill touch, with muffled comfort-hum,
A mind that in reply would mold
The depth it is emerging from.

My golden-white chrysanthemum
Blent solar heat and lunar cold—
The quiet which at night will come.

Perception keen, clear-thinking, plumb—
With welcomed will—the yet untold,
The depth it is emerging from.

The surface-breaking strength upswum
Knows height beyond the long-enscrolled,
The quiet which at night will come,
The depth it is emerging from.

Thoughts on "When light and silent time arrived"

The light and silent time may be the quiet dawn, or it may come when Sabbath-eve candles are lit and the Sabbath Queen is awaited, the Shekhinah, Hebrew name of the female emanative presence of the One. The latter possibility accords with the feeling that "For winter vim is honey hived"—light is borrowed from the day to greet the wisdom that enters from the depth in what might seem a colder or a darker time, the evening.

I like to think of the Sabbath candle flame as an eye with concentric colors. Touring the Middle East, I was struck by a carryover from the eye-charm of Egyptian god Horus to the ḥamsa, five-fingered amulet with eye in palm of hand. Concentric hues of the Sabbath flame have been interpreted as levels in the transcender's lifting-up to Wisdom.

What wisdom we might "gain" we get in order to spend and share. The sharing of the wisdom with us by the honey hived, by the light in dark, is the example of spending and sharing what we receive. We were never meant to hoard but only to give freely in the manner of the Lord Who is the Daybreak.

Sabbath wine is a "cordial," a heartener. It is an aid to the celebration of the soul's marriage with the Sabbath as embodiment of the Emanative Presence, or vital principle of the existent world. This deep belonging may let us feel, if not quite understand, the wedding of fate and freedom, of our destiny and our daily regenerated will to act. This matchmaking results from our acceptance of the summons made when the angel of potential speaks his name, which may become our own.

12 When light and silent time arrived

When light and silent time arrived
It loved things done but said, What more?
For winter vim is honey hived.

Let freedom have with fate connived:
You heard the name of what you're for
When light and silent time arrived.

Who find, not seek, have soul revived.
Health-widened lung will strength restore.
For winter vim is honey hived.

Your *ḥamsa* clay you'd find high-fived
That Lord- and Horus-eye adore
When light and silent time arrived.

The holy and *Shekhínah*-wived
The Sabbath wine with joy outpour.
For winter vim is honey hived.

We gain, not save, when we have strived.
The cordial was revealed at core
When light and silent time arrived.
For winter vim is honey hived.

Thoughts on "Chance object— pebble near the deep"

I'm expanding here one of my favorite ideas, the surrealist theme that "found objects" may stimulate our waking dream-life and galvanize writing or painting.

The expansion is on the level of depth: if the randomly found object opens the Unconscious, it is a key to unknown deeps. Sir Isaac Newton compared his scientific discoveries to mere seaside pebbles. William Wordsworth, studying the cloud bank spread out below him around Mt. Snowdon, looked at a hole in the white surface and all of a sudden began to hear the colossal roar of the waters below—deeps which had been sounding all the while, but could only now be heard!

Johann Wolfgang von Goethe, Germany's greatest poet, called his collected verse "occasional poetry"—written to suit an occasion. Traditionally the phrase meant sociable poems, a dedicatory epistle or letter of congratulation to a friend; but for the German poet, every poem he wrote was a response to whatever piqued his interest. Every topic, every question confronted was a found object with surreal (super-real) possibility.

Homer was "thalassal," or oceanic, in his depth, but one might say the Hellenic bard was himself the pebble tossed up by the Ocean of the Unmanifest, his superhuman capacity as unaccountable as the mystery from which it had emerged.

A more eye-catching Newtonian pebble or Wordsworthian cloud-gap is the rainbow that may by random tricks and odd angles of light crown the salty ocean, emblem of the Vergilian "tears of things." And finally, rhymes are found objects that lead the associative mind to unawaited places, quite in the way that startled Newton, Wordsworth, Homer by the suddenly apprehended roar of ocean surf.

13 Chance object—
pebble near the deep

Chance object—pebble near the deep:
That, Newton claimed, was all he found.
The Sea of Truth would secret keep.

Atop Mount Snowdon, ear would sleep
Till rift Will spied in cloud-bank ground.
Chance object—pebble near the deep.

See Goethe from occasion reap
The reams that compass him around:
The Sea of Truth would secret keep.

Though praise you on Ulysses heap,
Thalassal Homer wrote the sound.
Chance object—pebble near the deep.

Salt tears might *Mare Mater* weep,
Yet 'mid her waves we're rainbow-crowned.
The Sea of Truth would secret keep.

Each rhyme—mere shell in flowing sweep.
Yet surge may tidal soul astound.
Chance object—pebble near the deep.
The Sea of Truth would secret keep.

Thoughts on "For spectrum-sexuality"

Why is it that we can't decide whether our native country is fatherland or motherland? Not only do we have two parents, but since their roles overlap, each of these parental beings' natures will be doubled. "Male" and "female" appear biological categories, but what is manly or womanly behavior? A cultural construction, something imaginatively conceived.

Studying foreign languages will lead you to sexualities undreamt of and difficult to combine in any overarching schema. The sun is masculine in French (*le soleil*), feminine in German (*die Sonne*), neuter in Russian (*solntse*). The moon is feminine in French (*la lune*), masculine in German (*der Mond*), and either masculine or feminine in Russian (*mesiats* or *luná*). German poet Heinrich Heine tells of the female sun looking forward to the hugs of Poseidon when she'll descend into the Ocean. Would a French poet write of such a thing?

People who want to impose clear definitions and set rules for gender determination won't succeed, any more than tyrants can permanently incarcerate poets.

Schoolteachers don't mention that Shakespeare's "Shall I compare thee to a summer's day?" was one of the 39 sonnets where he speaks to his boyfriend before any woman is ever mentioned in the famous collection of 154 poems. People speculate about the identity of the "dark lady" of whom the poet is enamored, but it's the bisexuality of our ever-contemporary friend Will that, for most people, remains chiefly obscured. Every playwright, novelist, poet is androgynous to some degree in the life of body-mind, or else imaginings are imprisoned—intolerably so.

14 For spectrum-sexuality

For spectrum-sexuality
A debt we owe. In human speech
We gender everything we see,

Most foreign tongues will show. When we
A noun a gender grant, we reach
For spectrum-sexuality,

A realm where metaphors run free.
Male, female traits new-shaped they teach:
We gender everything we see.

Can self-defining creatures be
Constrained in how we picture each?
For spectrum-sexuality

Delight in beauty, headlong glee
Will fettered fearfulness impeach:
We gender everything we see.

To Will's dear boyfriend's rose the key:
"Spread forth your beauty!" he'd beseech.
For spectrum-sexuality
We gender everything we see.

Thoughts on "Let novel art-style rise in you"

"Revealings don't repeat": in the Sufic thought of Ibn Arabi, the disclosures of Essential Being to finite creatures are extremely brief and ever-altering. No disclosure will ever recur; a new one will come instead. Entire alertness will be required if you want to sense a new potential for poetic style arise in you.

Worship of ancestors, conformity to the preconceived, will limit openness to new disclosures. Risk appears along with openness, but go ahead and taste the rose (enjoy the moment of opening), and evade the rue (avoid ruefulness, remorse, regret for anything that doesn't work out for whatever reason).

In Buddhism we're cautioned against letting old movies automatically generate re-runs in the brain, blotting out life in favor of wearying, tedious tapes. Poet-artist William Blake viewed Imagination as the inhabitant of the house of which the windows are the beholder's eyes. You look through them, not with them. The "old movie" aspect of brain activity isn't a function but a dysfunction, filling up the present moment with unwanted past memories while nanosecond-quick disclosures of Essential Being go by unregarded.

The mind can blind the soul to art. It takes a heroic resolution to unclutter the brain from accumulated heaps of outdated films about a "you" that's past and gone. The feng shui or uncluttering must be comprehensive, and may be monumental.

15 Let novel art-style rise in you

Let novel art-style rise in you,
A realm of creatures life-endowed,
A way of being bravely new.

Revealings don't repeat. Askew
Are idols of the past, too proud.
Let novel art-style rise in you.

We're changed by minutes one or two.
They lose, who have to forebear bowed,
A way of being bravely new.

Though rose you taste, evade the rue.
The soul remorse will cripple, cowed.
Let novel art-style rise in you.

Old movies let the mind eschew.
Be cinema yourself, allowed
A way of being bravely new.

The hero heart would fain pursue
A singing wind, to psalming vowed.
Let novel art-style rise in you,
A way of being bravely new.

Thoughts on "A spectrum-length hate, love attain"

I've come to think of the spectrum as remedy for the label or the box. One isn't born to be a poet a scholar, or anything else. You are a continuum. Having been a scholar for 35 years didn't prevent me from turning into a full-time day-and-night poet upon retirement (or rather, resilement).

Every mental state contains its opposite, less or more clearly manifest. Bipolarism and manic-depressive syndrome are both misnomers, as I learn from specialist Kay Redfield Jameson. The two poles interact and affect each other intimately. The mode of heightened happiness is intermixed with manic agitation, exhilarating but fevered with a troubled, uncentered anxiety. And the sad mood is reckless when perilously abandoned-feeling.

To have a mentor-friend-rival gives you a chance for dialogue, and colloquy can put a solitary problem in perspective. My triply hyphenated word highlights the interpersonal continuum: a spectrum-range along which we move freely and flexibly between enmity and love.

If we think of the continuum as a landscape, we see the two opposites in each pair of contraries are sometimes apart, sometimes blended into the scenery.

We are creatures of Becoming, however much we seek fullness of Being. But the image-concept of the spectrum is our tool of rescue and reconciliation. Everything moves along a continuum: sexual orientations, world views, whatever foregrounds and backgrounds we use to compose our portrait and write our story.

16 A spectrum-length hate, love obtain

A spectrum-length hate, love obtain,
From hard to mild in changing mood,
Rest-move, win-fail—spread blent on plain.

'Tween glad refreshment, gloomy strain,
Devotion faithful, soul-woe feud,
A spectrum length hate, love obtain.

To follow, rival—friends might gain
Continuum for wooer, wooed:
Rest-move, win-fail—spread blent on plain.

Bipolarism pleasure, pain—
The sway, intense, will gauge elude:
A spectrum-length hate, love obtain.

From Southern Cross to Northern Wain
Are star-groups influence-imbued,
Rest-move, win-fail—spread blent on plain.

From Canis Major's dog-days' reign
To polar ray with cold endued,
A spectrum length hate, love obtain,
Rest-move, win-fail—spread blent on plain.

Thoughts on "How brief a time have I to say"

In an essay called "That to Philosophize Is to Learn How to Die" Michel de Montaigne wrote (in John Florio's translation): "Whatsoever I have to do before death, all leisure to end the same, seemeth short unto me, yea were it but of one hour." At age 90 my colleague and friend Katharina Mommsen said to me, "I don't take holidays; I haven't the time."

Trying to be as honest-ignorant as my mentor Socrates, I don't claim to convey more than merely truths of feeling. Yet, breathing in the sky of the Boundless to keep alive my center, the Heart, I'm always talking of the One, the wholeness I cannot know but only feel.

The tear of Jesus and the smile of Buddha are mutual correctives. How magisterial it may sound for an ignorant person to make inclusive judgments like that. But anyone buffeted by the winds of the Unbounded and unsettled by the flutterings of the Heart is entitled to a vision of the many-sidedness of the Manifold.

The myths we make embody our ever-restless, all-including nature. The poet Nikolay Gumilev in "Trees" could find Mary in the palm and Moses in the oak. I'll add Bacchus in the vine.

Goethe thought Muhammad banned wine among his followers because he wanted to be the only one who was drunk. But if all we know of the A and O, the Alpha and Omega, the beginning and the end, must come to us from our changeful nature, a bit of unsteadiness at the lovers' banquet cannot be amiss.

17 How brief a time have I to say

How brief a time have I to say
What sounded as from long ago,
Truth lasting that to mind made way.

The wisdom heard, which loved might stay
When honey-tongued in poet-flow,
How brief a time have I to say.

The wind and sun will shout Hurray,
The earth and stream, the A and O,
Truth lasting that to mind made way.

I'd Christ-tear, Buddha-smile portray:
That both can light the way we grow
How brief a time have I to say.

We're tragicomic human play
Of jocoserious glee-woe,
Truth lasting that to mind made way.

O Mary, Moses, Bacchus, ray
Of grace on these my lines let glow:
How brief a time have I to say
Truth lasting that to mind made way.

Thoughts on "The science mind, the will to verse"

I view the Eden Trees of Knowledge and Life as growing from a single root. So art and science, there, are equally affirmed. At the end of William Blake's epic of psychology, *The Four Zoas,* on the new earth facing the new heaven rise Bacon, Newton, and Locke to face Milton, Shakespeare, and Chaucer.

Like the Sun that shines on both, art and science ought not to hoard but freely scatter ("asperse") their complementary benefits. A simple, homey thought: without central heating and an electric fan I couldn't write poetry in comfort. Gratitude for these I gladly combine with my general gratitude for breathing.

Art and science are both at risk under a tyranny of greed, such as now strives to consolidate power. Eight men earn as much as do half the population of the planet. One percent of the people in the US have as much wealth as the lower 40 percent of the people as a whole. When I wrote "Heart never hoards," I wanted to envision a rainbow above the flood of avarice.

The verse I'm trying to comment upon in a useful way partly eludes my re-creative powers right now, for the outward conditions of all our lives are ever more unsettling. Money is in control, and it desires nothing but more money. The apple of temptation in the Bible, the apple of discord in the tale of the Trojan War, are myths of decline and fall that refuse to fade.

18 The science mind, the will to verse

The science mind, the will to verse
Can, wise, combined, an eden be.
Cool airy current may asperse

The motor fan: we bold immerse
Twin feelings in felicity—
The science mind, the will to verse.

A hymn of culture I rehearse
That nature aids: when they agree
Cool airy current may asperse

The rhapsode pair, the double nurse
Of twinned awareness. Praise then we
The science mind, the will to verse.

Heart never hoards—from heaven purse
Came generous the energy
Cool airy current may asperse.

In wording terse with cupid thyrse
I sing, and spring, while happily
The science mind, the will to verse
Cool airy current may asperse.

Thoughts on "How fine to feel you needn't bow"

Pangloss, or All-tongue, was the name of the cartoon professor in Voltaire's *Candide* (also a rollicking musical by Leonard Bernstein) who taught that all is for the best in this best of all possible worlds. I'm trying to keep sober in my service of Hellenic Pan, the God of All, by reining in a naturally cheerful train of fanciful thought. I'm also grateful for the chance to "let my garden grow."

I don't propose a philosophic optimism, rather a mentality that follows the concept of "dao" (often spelled "tao" but pronounced "dow"), the peaceful Chinese practice of acceding to the rhythms of Nature. In this regard I like to think of Goethe's couplet: "How splendid the heritage, never scant! / Time is my wealth and my field to plant."

When I retired I made a promise to myself: I would write a sonnet, or equally exacting craft-poem, every day of my life so long as the body-mind would allow. This gives me the farmer-feeling the German poet embodied in two perfect lines: each day I sow an art work in the field of human culture as it evolves with time and the seasons. (Goethe's lyric is poem 100 in his *West-East Divan,* which I translated in 2010.)

A related discipline of mindfulness, for daily contentment, that I carried out as father of a growing child was to keep a detailed diary of that process of growth. I memorized conversations, and they're recorded in the volumes now for me to look at and to bring back moments of humor, pathos, and surprise during the time from ages 1 to 18 of my daughter's life. The total work, written first on manual typewriter, then on computer, is probably longer than Boswell's biography of Samuel Johnson. I'd call it *Phenomenology of Everyday Life.*

19 How fine to feel you needn't bow

How fine to feel you needn't bow
To judgment of a wealthy boss
Nor others' mood to rule allow.

The four-directional kowtow
I'll not perform, to moral loss.
How fine to feel you needn't bow.

My guide let be the deeper dao,
And worries vain away I'll toss
Nor others' mood to rule allow.

No pearls I throw before the sow
Nor bear the weight of olden cross.
How fine to feel you needn't bow.

My seed within my field I plow,
Nor wail the guilt-rid albatross,
Nor others' mood to rule allow.

My right will higher grace allow,
Unhyphenated Pan, no -gloss.
How fine to feel you needn't bow
Nor others' mood to rule allow.

Thoughts on "I thank you, kind electric fan"

Here's the kind of poem a man writes who studies with pleasure what I just called the phenomenology of everyday life. The polysyllable derives from the Greek verb "to appear." We record what appears to us, what we experience. Until I became a father I never cared to keep a diary, but Sarah by her alert originality and sprightly gladness taught me the value of remembering the wonders of each day.

As you keep track of the revelations of mere appearance, unembellished daily facts of living, you find they grow vastly in appeal, since recording is a kind of art. And the journal is mimesis, imitation of the real in the word, if ever an art form was.

That is why I reference a comment in the Islamic hadith or memoir literature, reporting Muhammad's perception about God: Walk to the Lord and He will run to you. Resolve to record moments that matter, and they will multiply, rushing in so fast you will barely keep up with them in your hours of most rapid typing. You'll enjoy, too, an awakening of the half-dormant arts of memory when you note conversations that shouldn't be "forgot and never brought to mind."

Sarah, in the elevator at Boscov's department store: "My bed is a elevator." (I transcribe it the way she said it.)

Dad: "Why is that?"

Sarah: "Because the elevator changes the floor and my bed changes the time of day."

Or the moment can be wordless. Watching the last of the Sabbath candle flames go out, Sarah began to cry.

20 I thank you, kind electric fan

I thank you, kind electric fan,
By which I sing my villanelles,
Love doing what I find I can.

I've passed the olden mortal span
Whereof outdated scripture tells:
I thank you, kind electric fan.

My evening life I, Adam man,
Make heaven, leave unneeded hells,
Love doing what I find I can.

I walked to One, to me that ran.
Our friendship overwhelms, upwells.
I thank you, kind electric fan.

Horizon when I grateful scan
I find the sky more bright than bells,
Love doing what I find I can.

For Wind's a Spirit, and the clan
Named Poet know the best of spells.
I thank you, kind electric fan,
Love doing what I find I can.

Thoughts on "Each moment's matter I can mold"

Each art offers a temporal dimension: the eye makes a journey as it travels around a painting, and every musical score will graph a structuring of time. Alert focus will catch the making of nanosecond sculpture by a wave or squirrel.

Homer, prototype of the master-poet, writes in tidal time when the short and long syllables make their recurrent hexameter patterns while he's telling a story (long-short-short being the rhythm unit sounded six times per line). Using a one-time word I found in the *Oxford English Dictionary,* I call the *Odyssey* and *Iliad* poluphloisboisterous, a condensation of poluphoisboian (many-voiced) and boisterous. (James Joyce might have said "manyboiced," or even "manyboyced" to work his own name into a whimsy-word.) "Multivocal" is the Greek poet's recurrent way of depicting the sea.

The spatial analogues of musical tone are of equally vivid interest. A "timbre" (pronounced "tamber") is a tone color. Some people see hues when they hear tunes.

The bird's egg blue I mention is a way to indicate the lightened sky. Every defined vocal range, each musical instrument, is an imaginative way of fixing for repeated enjoyment a set of tone colors. Languages structure colors variedly in verbal classification patterns. In Russian there's no word for blue: you're obliged to select either light blue (*goluboi*) or indigo (*sinii*)—robin's egg or navy.

Given the intertwinings of the audible and visual worlds of perception, each moment's matter is atmosphere, spatial and temporal, earthy and airy.

21 Each moment's matter I can mold

Each moment's matter I can mold.
There's not a one need pass me by,
Should mind love's deep attention hold.

By sheet-of-music graph we're told
How structured tone though time will fly:
Each moment's matter I can mold.

A sculptured wave is air-enscrolled:
Make time a statue standing nigh,
Should mind love's deep attention hold.

The verse-realm wealth was known of old,
Poluphloisboisterous and spry:
Each moment's matter I can mold.

Jade-rare, more radiant than gold,
What timbres land from Hand on high,
Should mind love's deep attention hold.

Through bird's-egg blue, in wood and wold,
We gather hues, their truth descry.
Each moment's matter I can mold
Should mind love's deep attention hold.

Thoughts on "In value realms inventive be"

Goodness, beauty, and truth may possibly converge, as Plato hoped, and certainly they interact. Aristotle's morality of moderation, avoiding both deficiency and excess to achieve a golden mean, brings to mind the Greek ideal of symmetric balance in architecture and statuary. Both the ideally good person living in the world and the ideally represented one in a sculpture by Phidias or Praxiteles are at once beautiful and morally instructive.

Morality and truth can have an equally fruitful relation. Immanuel Kant's "categorical imperative" or absolute, inviolable principle of morality (a variant of the golden rule), is deepened when the truths of the unconscious revealed in dreams make it clear that the imperative is an expression of the superego, valid in its partial function though not as a complete account of ethical obligation.

A captain at the ship's helm, my metaphor of the free spirit inventive in the realm of values, is ancient: it appears in Greek as *Philosophia bioi kybernetes,* Love of wisdom the helmsman of life, abbreviated as phi beta kappa.

The successful visual or musical artist fashions not only the art work but the standard of judgment by which the work is to be judged. The lifestyle artist shows new ethical principles, or novel applications of older ones, that in turn will influence any future philosophic ethics. The scientist opens up a realm of truth and beauty that earlier ages could envision only as miraculous: what could be more wise and lovelier than a heart transplant?

22 In value realms inventive be

In value realms inventive be,
Both apt to teach and deft to learn,
Grasp helm as captain, steadily.

Pre-active to transvalue, we
A world may shape that love shall earn:
In value realms inventive be.

Let eyes in you a scripture see
That can the sky enfold, not spurn:
Grasp helm as captain, steadily.

The body and the spirit free
Of separation to discern,
In value realms inventive be.

In minutes live contentedly
While set for yonder aim to yearn:
Grasp helm as captain, steadily.

Be turned toward eternity,
Flame seraph-like to shine, not burn,
In value realms inventive be:
Grasp helm as captain, steadily.

Thoughts on "Another villaneller-man"

The word "villaneller-man" came to me from a memory of my teaching days when I'd bring a tambourine to class to demonstrate the pleasures of poetic meter.

I'd tell the students they were welcome to call me "Mr. Tambourine Man" after the musician in the Bob Dylan song.

A curious thing: while regular meters have gradually vanished from the works of poets, the beat that distinguishes them has been (over)amplified in rock music, and more recently strong beats have come back in hip hop. Return of the repressed?

My quotation comes from a hadith or memoir narrative about the Prophet Muhammad, not from the Qur'an itself: "Allah is beautiful and He loves beauty." Interestingly, the Marmaduke Pickthall translation of the Islamic scripture is filled with strong, and strongly effective rhythms, helping to make it into one of the great works of English literature.

Turning from Bob Dylan to Dylan Thomas, the much-admired villanelle "Do not go gentle into that good night" written by that poet (who never reached the age of 40) appears the work of a youthful-minded speaker. Why should we "rage against the dying of the light" if that dying brings on a night that is admittedly "good"? The point of the poem is to embody an impulse, not to present a logical argument.

Better to sing than rage. When William Blake faced death, he sang hymns of his own composition, reportedly so loud they shook the walls (see poem 28).

23 Another villaneller-man

Another villaneller-man,
Competitor with Dylan T.,
Will write some lines you'll like to scan.

I'm sure he's welcome, there's no ban.
You must have known there soon would be
Another villaneller-man.

The speaker of the vast Qur'an
Said God 'loves beauty.' Therefore we
Will write some lines you'll like to scan.

Since Alexander and Roxanne
Both Greek and Persian hope to see
Another villaneller-man.

From Vestal to Afghanistan
The folk who care for melody
Will write some lines you'll like to scan.

Of Dylan Thomas I'm a fan,
But time moves on, let's all agree:
Another villaneller-man
Will write some lines you'll like to scan.

Thoughts on "The vasty volume I peruse"

The book I'm envisioning in this poem could easily be a proof-book of my own: the problem described is one I try to solve, over and over, yet never can dismiss.

It is the problem of pet words we didn't know we had. The jinns, or little spirit imps, delight to mock the thing we love the most. If I'm carried away by the luck of having sung something right, the little devil will sneak into my lines one of his puckish, prankish pet words.

Where does he get them? The example of another writer with the same jinn issue may answer for us.

In a book I've been reading the author writes "fierce" and "pragmatic" (plus their variants in noun or adverb) every few pages. And thus he offers the key that we were seeking: the pet word is a variant of the Freudian slip. It comes from the unconscious, the dream world, to reveal something central to your being, but which you hadn't wanted so blatantly to disclose.

24 The vasty volume I peruse

The vasty volume I peruse
Contains, whatever else 'twill say,
Pet words he'll certainly reuse.

Pragmatic—term he likes to choose,
And *fierce*. The will must have its way.
The vasty volume I peruse—

Self-portraiture! We win and lose.
They're lively—maybe they're okay,
Pet words he'll certainly reuse.

Yet mannered habit will amuse.
For such recurrence, wait! I pray
The vasty volume I peruse.

Unwitting, 'twill my wish refuse,
Nor ever can our friend delay
Pet words he'll certainly reuse.

Pragmatic, fierce—we *get* it! Booze
No better sketch would help portray
The vasty volume I peruse,
Pet words he'll certainly reuse.

Thoughts on "A spectrum ethic shall we state?

In the thoughts on #18, "A spectrum-length hate, love obtain," I noted the spectrum-like nature of my every thought, mood, state of being. Here I ask, How can we base an ethical attitude on this recognition?

Freud liberated the world of night for me when he assured his reader that there's no guilt involved in anything we dream. The unconscious is unfamiliar with morality: it works through problems by expressing wish and fear, usually both at once. It's usually a relief to get up in the morning after working on these things all night.

No guilt in dreaming? Then if dream-thought, energy and motive from the unconscious, exerts power throughout our waking hours as well, these impulses and intimations are also free and cannot be impugned. They might need to be regulated or treated with discretion and wisdom, but in themselves they are not evil.

Again, the spectrum is the key: every moment of waking life is a continuum of awareness that can be anywhere on the line between the poles of pure logic and pure irrationality. If you want to love your neighbor as yourself, you have to love yourself. And that's easier to do in a world where imagination is evaluated in loving empathy, helped by our spectrum guide.

"Halidom" is an older word for holiness. It is, in the ode by Friedrich Schiller set to music by Beethoven, the *Heiligtum* of our *Freude,* the sacred domain of our joy. *Freude* is akin to *Freiheit*, or freedom, the shedding of needless guilt.

25 A spectrum ethic shall we state?

A spectrum ethic shall we state?
From sick to well—continuum.
Guilt-guileless—open road, no gate.

We diagnose, and estimate
What data show when questions come.
A spectrum ethic shall we state?

What lessons let us formulate
Depends on where we're heading from.
Guilt-guileless—open road, no gate.

A child it pays not to berate:
Unknown whence budding thoughts have swum.
A spectrum ethic shall we state?

Then don't condemn, be pensive, wait:
With big unknowns the mind goes numb.
Guilt-guileless—open road, no gate.

Who love not self must others hate.
In neighbor's heart glimpse halidom.
A spectrum ethic shall we state?
Guilt-guileless—open road, no gate.

Thought on "The light through gauzy curtain glows"

A friend brought me a bouquet of flowers for my 70th birthday, and almost 4 years later I continue to look at it daily. No stem or leaf is hurt. The petals dim a bit, but that is all.

A new work of art had come into being: an emblem not of springtime youth but of autumnal power to enliven. The bouquet stands next to a bookcase owned by my late father, of blessed memory. The door-glass looks wavy and stream-like, having been slowly flowing downward all these many years. Glass may be called a liquid in suspension, and the old-fashioned kind shows the gradual travel.

Dead blooms perdure, dead glass flows yet. Gauzy light through translucent drapery mellows the phenomenon, altering the style of the visual art. The reflections in the bookcase doors are dreamlike now, with a flowing, molten light I've seen in works by Arshile Gorky.

My father David Bidney made his early reputation with his Guggenheim Fellowship book *The Psychology and Ethics of Spinoza,* still in print today. The calm Jewish philosopher of the 17th century might have liked the scene I portray. Dead things, for him, lived always in the Universal Mind, which was at the same time Universal Matter. An intellectual love of this God, maintained in perfect equanimity, was the deepest joy that could be known. My father was calm in that way. His final words were tranquil and accepting. He said, "Take me."

26 The light through gauzy draping glows

The light through gauzy draping glows
And brings to life a dead bouquet
And sheer delight of being shows.

Sun gently soft, the highs and lows
Deploying, can with petals play.
The light through gauzy draping glows.

With dream-distorted curving flows
Half-molten glass of olden day
And sheer delight of being shows.

My father's ancient bookcase knows
The trivial goes, the depth will stay:
The light through gauzy draping glows.

He wrote of calm Spinoza. Woes
The mind outgrows with no dismay
And sheer delight of being shows.

You taught me love for wisdom, rose
Of many-layered fragrant Way.
The light through gauzy draping glows
And sheer delight of being shows.

Thoughts on "The coffee speeds my breathing up"

Coffee is for me the elixir of Eos (Greek), also called Aurora (Latin), deity of dawn. Dew is the goddess' tears: does she cry out of longing for love? Hellenic myth ascribes to her many lovers, and Aphrodite had indeed given her the curse (?) of being perpetually in love after she lay with Ares, the war god to whom the Lady of Passion was always extra-maritally attracted.

Speed of work tempo is appropriate here, for the dawn-bearing horses are swift. Coffee and singing are each a "sweet entrée" or entrance into a time of energy and vigor. I feel daily at the service of a divinity who offers, via the dream-world, the driving commands. I'm the minstrel, the jongleur—medieval French singer-acrobat with a name related to our word "juggler."

The romance of Eos with Tithonus proved a farce, for the latter, asking for immortality, forgot to request that it be accompanied by immortal *youth*. Aging and decrepit, he found little to enjoy when the hoped-for gift was granted.

This will not happen to me because, living in an age that no longer lauds epic heroes in song, I'll have to emulate Odysseus and Homer both, so far as I can manage that. The conquest of time by verse will replace the blinding of Cyclops—and a good thing, too: far rather would I be the latest David.

27 The coffee speeds my breathing up

The coffee speeds my breathing up,
That Time with hurried pulse might say,
Write, minstrel! Sing before you sup.

More eager I than sprightly pup,
Compliant wagtail, cry, Hurray!
The coffee speeds my breathing up—

My stash of rhymes I'd better dup,
Set agile grammar-strength in play:
Write, minstrel! Sing before you sup.

We'll quickly stride a-marching: hup!
ROTC—the army way—
The coffee speeds my breathing up.

Reward: fine panfish, maybe scup
From Mass., the Narragansett Bay:
Write, minstrel! Sing before you sup.

Now, aren't you glad you sang? (Say: Yup!)
Jongleurs prefer a sweet entrée.
The coffee speeds my breathing up.
Write, minstrel! Sing before you sup.

Thoughts on "When Blake was dying, loud he sang"

I picture the deathbed hymn of Blake (reportedly composed by him) as marrying earth to heaven, in line with the poet's own habitual practice: all three of his psychological epic poems have happy endings (to phrase it mildly) of world transformation when the doors of perception are opened. *Jerusalem, Milton,* and (best of the three) *The Four Zoas* are filled with strife and havoc, but they cannot be allowed to end until the problems are resolved in prophetic vision.

At the same time, the *Zoas* will recall the defeat of the serpent in Genesis, of Satan in Revelation. For although Blake was above all a poet of mental synthesis (from whom Carl Jung borrowed hugely), he had a strong awareness of the threat, within his own mind daily, of the Spirit that denies.

The forces that create mental tensions—Passion, Intellect, Intuition, and Loving Imagination—work in pairs of creative contraries, and the pairs are themselves creative contraries. Wild Passion is mildened by receptive Intuition; assertive Intellect learns the limits of logic through Imagination. Each member of a creative pair is guided by the maxim "Opposition is true friendship."

That's true so long as the opposition is one of creative contrariety, not destructive nihilation. Revenge, the will to destroy for the sake of an over-prized ego, can threaten life and might destroy our planet. Goethe's term for the destructive will, the "Spirit that denies," mirrors the Blakean term "Negation." To distinguish creative contrariety from annihilating negativity is our task in moral life. Ironically and sadly, Blake never finished *The Four Zoas*. We have it in manuscript.

28 When Blake was dying, loud he sang

While Blake was dying, loud he sang:
Surrounding walls began to shake,
And all with laud of heaven rang.

'Tis written that Mount Sinai sprang
Apart in trembling, frightful quake.
While Blake was dying, loud he sang.

Defeated, crushed, the rebel fang
By sacred feet that trod the snake—
And all with laud of heaven rang.

Be praised, that made the sky-bells clang!
Warm dawn-embrace at morning-break!
While Blake was dying, loud he sang.

Earth married sky, as yin the yang:
They loved the hymn composed by Blake—
And all with laud of heaven rang.

The Devil wept—old woe re-stang:
The rock was reft, made waters wake.
While Blake was dying, loud he sang,
And all with laud of heaven rang.

Thoughts on "What made the world's unmanifest"

    Evident to everyone is the idea that whatever force brought Something into being where Nothing-at-All might have continued forever is a power both manifest or palpable (since we're alive) and unmanifest (since we know nothing about it). An existent being is only a metaphor of what's never manifested, embodying and putting forth the creative power of it while never knowing what it is.

    As metaphors of the unknown, we can't understand ourselves. The injunction admired by Socrates, "Know yourself," quoted from the inscription in the temple courtyard at Delphi, is unfulfillable, though it may be good to try, so as to test your limit. Ibn Arabi, renowned Sufi thinker, suggested that when the Bible said we are created in the image of God it meant that we are like Him in having both manifest and unmanifest qualities to our nature. Metaphors of the unknowable, we're largely in the dark to ourselves.

    But what a wonder now appears. The unknown power that moves the world from nothingness into being has a being, a nature, that is to us unmanifest, though metaphorically clarified in an oblique and always partial, finite way by the metaphors that we are and make. The unmanifest nature of that power is a wonderment and a mystery and a joy to think about in its greatness and unfathomable depth-height.

    But I am thinking now of what may be a greater wonder still. We have the unmanifest within us. We can never know our true depth, our essential being, for we are creatures of Becoming who live in Time. Yet how godly that Unmanifest!

29 What made the world's unmanifest

What made the world's unmanifest,
The beings each a metaphor.
We less have known than yet we've guessed.

'Tis claimed that we're uniquely blest
In mirroring the Unknown More.
What made the world's unmanifest.

How *know yourself*? We fail the test,
Our soul unshown by mortals' lore:
We less have known than yet we've guessed.

Through teachings of the east and west
Mind seeks an ocean void of shore:
What made the world's unmanifest.

With ignorance of depth confessed,
In heart the darkness we restore:
We less have known than yet we've guessed.

Let dark the over-light speak best:
Not silent, then, the ocean roar.
What made the world's unmanifest:
We less have known than yet we've guessed.

Thoughts on "Had fear of silence never cried"

You cry in a time of crisis, a word that derives from the Greek *krisis*, the turning point in a disease. Rudolf Otto found in the "holy" an energy both menacing and fascinating. The crisis I went through had both qualities.

Had I not been terrified of carpal tunnel syndrome, of its power to stop my violin playing for weeks on end, I wouldn't have been driven in despair to make word music by translating the most intricately exacting and sweetest Russian lyric I know, "Love" by Vyacheslav Ivanov. When I saw and heard the verbal melody emerge upon the page, I realized a new life had begun.

Rainer Maria Rilke, a Qur'an reader, wrote in the first of his *Duino Elegies* that "Every angel terrifies." Crises are frightful: think of the struggle of Muhammad to escape the mountain cave where the angel tried to wrestle him into submission so he'd recite the Qur'an. The illiterate Prophet thought the overforce had been an evil genie, playing a devilish trick. The agony he felt recalls what Jacob must have gone through in his own laming fight with an angelic spirit.

But Muhammad received the Qur'an, and Jacob received a new identity—Israel, the struggler with God. Carpal tunnel (from which I recovered after five weeks of hourly hand exercise) proved to be the Angel of Word Music. Muhammad hadn't known he could read under the right (heaven-induced) conditions, nor did I know I could become a poet. I had been taught that Milton, Shelley, Coleridge were all of them "geniuses," and what was that? A burden word meant to convince "ordinary" folk that we must take a back seat on the spirit bus that rides through time.

30 Had fear of silence never cried

Had fear of silence never cried
Relief! Sing sweet! Write poetry!
I'd even yet in prose abide.

Aye, tunnel syndrome vainly tried
Enchainment. I'd remain unfree
Had fear of silence never cried.

*Pray, put your violin aside
Until complete recovery.*
I'd even yet in prose abide

Had angel tune not doom defied
And lyric words not urged—ah me!
Had fear of silence never cried

I'd not have heard that voice, and I'd
Mute poet stay, and dolor dree:
I'd even yet in prose abide.

Had life-lines lover-tongued not sighed
I'd not have fallen, weak of knee.
Had fear of silence never cried
I'd even yet in prose abide.

Thoughts on "My life shows naught has higher claim"

Mystical Sufi writers, culminating in Ibn Arabi, made two discoveries. (1) Religions or creeds, myths or beliefs, are all containers, each a glass lending color, or a cup lending form, to flowing spirit. (2) The Platonic Forms, ideals of art and life since Greco-Roman times, shouldn't be regarded as cold abstractions in a postmortal heaven. Rather, they are the 99 Names of God as found in the Qur'an, rubrics of heavenly potential waiting to be actualized by you and me on earth.

Unmanifest potentials in the Originating Power can summon you to mobilize what lay unmanifest in your own divine being. The Angel speaks the Name, designates the potential, that you can realize and fulfil, even though you may never have dreamed it possible.

The strong appeal of this idea lies largely in the multiplicity of the Names and the possibility, even likelihood, that you'll be alerted to several of them in succession. You may potentially have, and actually acquire, several identities, one after the other.

The idea of Wisdom arising from the Unmanifest relates to prophetic intuitions in your dreams. The poet-playwright Shelley in *Prometheus Unbound* shows Asia, the heroine of the drama, descending to Demogorgon, the black sun or dark radiance of the deep Unconscious, in a quest to comprehend herself, the world, and the connection between them.

What does the Sun of Darkness tell? That Love is the origin and goal of all our being. He tells the spelunker of the world of Night what she had always darkly known.

31 My life shows naught has higher claim

My life shows naught has higher claim
To welcome, rightly understood:
Be summoned by your secret Name.

From your Unmanifest there came
So far a merely partial good.
My life shows naught has higher claim

Your best potential yet to frame:
If you'd but let it come, it would.
Be summoned by your secret Name.

Chance may too soon your wildness tame,
Too softened make your hardihood.
My life shows naught has higher claim

Than call to what you are. 'Tis blame
When stunted thought says ought and should.
Be summoned by your secret Name.

The seraph dwelt in heaven flame:
Alerted by the Word, he could.
My life shows naught has higher claim:
Be summoned by your secret Name.

Thoughts on "A single villanelle, no more"

We likely all remember Dylan Thomas' "Do not go gentle into that good night." Equally, I love Theodore Roethke's "I wake to sleep, and take my waking slow," and Elizabeth Bishop's "The art of losing isn't hard to master."

Such poems are rare, and why? We're taught implicitly that we ought to fear them. I heard an undergraduate creative writing major sigh, "I hope to be worthy of writing a sonnet some day." I often hear this timid attitude toward intricate forms of poetry.

Nursery rhymes and Dr. Seuss and the tuneful words of Sesame Street remain in the minds of children, to their lasting delight. If kids aren't scared of hearing and reciting regular, resounding rhythms, what would be daunting in the offer that they, too, might compose in singable verse?

I want kids in grade school to try villanelles. Chinese children write poems in traditional forms. When Boris Pasternak declaimed lyrics of his own for Russian troops during the Second World War, he noticed the soldiers forming each word silently along with him. Crafted artisanal verse livens, leavens the heart and brings you into the being of word music, the place I dwell and dally and delay.

32 A single villanelle, no more

A single villanelle, no more,
Have Thomas, Roethke, Bishop writ.
Why not vast lyric flood outpour?

It is a form that I adore
And many morns devote to it.
A single villanelle, no more,

Falls short of what a poet's for—
An ecstasy, a frenzy-fit!
Why not vast lyric flood outpour?

In wind the seed and spoor and spore
Of villanelle-potentials flit.
A single villanelle, no more,

I think a mediocre score.
Bestir yourself, and work a bit!
Why not vast lyric flood outpour?

Poetic strength, good folk, restore
Where Pegasus, aloft, alit.
A single villanelle, no more—
Why not vast lyric flood outpour?

Thoughts on "We cheer achievers apt at sport"

"I'm going out for Petrarchan next semester—just got my letter in sestinas." I wrote my sentence on the pattern of those I've heard spoken by young athletes about basketball or football.

I've been trying out lately for new poetic sports, at times even inventing a few. My "slimmed-down fourteeners with four-beat lines and tight, sweet harmonies" (subtitle of a book) add tight sweetness to their tone-accords when, a hundred times, only two rhyme-endings are allowed per lyric poem. I think of it as a new kind of track event.

If you translate intricately shaped verse from other languages you become aware of other sound patterns than Americans usually hear. The French and Germans like the six-beat sonnet, while our Shakespeare generally writes in fives. Russians love three-syllable meters, rhythm schemes based on variedly accented triplets, and I borrow this idea freely when I want rapid motion and revved-up energy.

I practice my craft-rhythm events, the way athletes drill and try out tactics on the field. I learn new forms by writing them in sets of a hundred.

Sometimes a master-poet will be my master craftsman, and I'll emulate his verse forms in "replies" while rendering his works, as I did with Friedrich Rückert when I dialogued with him in *The Boundless and the Beating Heart*.

I compete as folk fiddler, too: last week I entered a contest and sang a ballad with fiddle accompaniment: "Black Jack Davy." I made semi-finals! Better yet, I wrote three poems—about preparing, playing, and style choice.

33 We cheer achievers apt at sport

We cheer achievers apt at sport,
Be-laureling the athlete-skill.
Go, toss the ball to poets' court!

To competition-bliss exhort
The shouters that arenas fill:
We cheer achievers apt at sport.

Is verse a last and bad resort?
Bestir, my friends, the lyric will:
Go, toss the ball to poets' court.

What toxins lyric drive abort?
Why limpness, apathetic ill?
We cheer achievers apt at sport.

Each op*port*unity's a port—
Sail on, nor ever fear a spill.
Go, toss the ball to poets' court.

Praise fortitude of every sort:
Ascend we then Olympus-hill!
We cheer achievers apt at sport:
Go, toss the ball to poets' court.

Thoughts on "Who love sweet tone shall never die"

Playful whimsy is the keynote here. "The while the birds in air stream by"? Why not write "While birds alert in air stream by"? What does "the while" mean?

I put it in just for fun, to echo earlier times. "The while" means "while" and nothing more, but it recalls the practice of keeping the beat going strong by inserting a meter-filling syllable. I'm thinking of the gravedigger's song in *Hamlet*: "Oh, a pickaxe and a spade, a spade, / For and a shrouding sheet! / Oh a pit of clay for to be made / For such a guest is meet!" "For and"? "For to be made?" The "For" is both times a meter-keeper. Those were the days when a song was a song, a tune with a beat, and you never forgot it.

In the same whimsical way I wrote, "Treat gawkers to a hawkish cry." This time I'm thinking of Walt Whitman's line, "I sound my barbaric yawp over the roofs of the world." That line is itself a playful invention: "i SOUND my barBARic YAWP O-ver the ROOFS of the WORLD" is a six-beat line mainly in three-beat rhythm units, a slightly rough dactylic hexameter, meter of the master-epics of Western civilization: *Iliad, Odyssey, Aeneid, The Nature of Things*.

Another little bit of sun comes with the stuntmanship of constructing analogous adverbs that don't yet quite exist. If we legitimately say "afar," why not "anear"? And why not still another logically allowable oddity—"anigh"?

The last quatrain contains a smiling memory: "jangle-belled," remolded from Bob Dylan's "In the jingle-jangle morning I'll be following you."

34 Who love sweet tone shall never die

Who love sweet tone shall never die
But be of heaven hand upheld
The while the birds in air stream by.

Come fly, dear friend, let's you and I
Feel sound and light their forces meld:
Who love sweet tone shall never die.

All flights are up, yet underlie
Your course the drives by wind unfelled
The while the birds in air stream by.

Treat gawkers to a hawkish cry,
Be godly rivals will-impelled:
Who love sweet tone shall never die.

Afar becomes anear, anigh
As ear and eye see, hear enspelled
The while the birds in air stream by.

Divine, the mind will bear us high
Beyond cathedrals jangle-belled:
Who love sweet tone shall never die
The while the birds in air stream by.

Thoughts on "The dark is not the Nil at all"

The major insight here is owed to my favorite medieval thinker, Ibn Arabi. Poets have so often equated night and death—Walt Whitman does this continually, in strongly affecting poems—that one may easily forget the equation is not inevitable and may even grievously mislead.

Night takes place in time, which lives and moves. Night flows—it is more the Nile than the Nil. Night may be invoked as a metaphor, a symbol, for a state of dark unknowing, but that state—like night itself—is not void: it is our lives. The Being of the Source, whatever one may call it, is unknowable, indefinable. So if it is reflected in its results only symbolically, only as an oblique and partly opaque intimation, all our knowledge of those results or effects of the creative Power is incomplete and metaphoric.

I next compare night to the silence in a hall, which is not true silence any more than the darkness of night is true nullity. Our ears comfort us with a steady whispering, something between a sibilance and a hum, that wards off true silence, which would terrify, as it would be deathlike, void-like. Instead, what we hear is only a metaphor of silence, a thing that intimates it but isn't the same. Silence and night can be metaphors of death, but to serve as metaphor they are not identical with it but rather point to it. They point metaphorically beyond themselves.

Metaphors emblemize death to a degree, but also guard against it. Time itself is a metaphor of this kind: it points beyond itself, to eternity, but makes life possible in our only partial darkness, which is visible, not void.

35 The dark is not the Nil at all

The dark is not the Nil at all:
The Naught one fears we cannot see,
Nor need the night our mind appall.

We Nile Unflowable may call
The Nil Unknowable—no "e."
The dark is not the Nil at all.

It points beyond the knowledge wall
That can't be passed by such as we,
Nor need the night our mind appall.

'Tis like the silence in a hall
Where softness made of tone must be:
The dark is not the Nil at all.

Through metaphor we death forestall:
Mere time's not quite eternity,
Nor need the night our mind appall.

Slow time, still night—pure signs befall
The seeker wanting imagery.
The dark is not the Nil at all,
Nor need the night our mind appall.

Thoughts on "You need to change your name within"

Here is the Sufi mystical thought regarding Names: they are invigoratingly changeable divine guides to stages of Being in our Becoming.

After his laming wrestle with the angel, Jacob was renamed Israel, the Struggler with God. The parable is my favorite prototype for the act of renewal as in part renaming.

Ibn Arabi has told a Sufi emblem-story to show how disconcerting, even crazed-making, such a transforming encounter may be. A prince who is enjoying a social evening with friends no longer appears to be present in mind. He doesn't hear what anyone says but, with blank eyes, may be attending to something else—we know not what. Does he look upset? happy? confused? He can't say a word about it, not being in a position to clarify.

He has been listening to the voice of his royal father, the commander-in-chief, who is calling on him to undertake an unexpected mission.

He is turning into someone else, having heard his own new "Name." Perhaps it will be a permanent "identity" for him, but don't count on it. The word "identity" is a problem, as it derives from Latin *idem*, meaning "same." Early on, we're each given a "name," and folk suppose that it indicates our "identity," something about us that will remain reliably steady and unchanging. When Jacob turned into Israel he showed just how misleading such assumptions can be. If you want, or even if you don't, you may acquire another "identity" at any moment.

36 You need to change your name within

You need to change your name within,
As Jacob Israël became,
Embraved initiative to win.

You well might feel your vision spin,
All objects altered, shaky frame—
You need to change your name within

So doubt may finish, faith begin.
Hark, therefore, to a heart-voiced aim,
Embraved initiative to win.

Withdraw yourself, no chaos-din
Admit: stay calm and free of blame:
You need to change your name within.

We're each to angel-mind akin
When given tidings to proclaim,
Embraved initiative to win.

Flee Latin *idem*'s evil grin!
"Iden-tity" don't keep the "same":
You need to change your name within,
Embraved initiative to win.

Thoughts on "Indignant ire is anger all the same"

Anger's the unintended self-punishment of the angry. It has been likened to swallowing a bottle of poison intended for an enemy. I've felt the effect—it destroys me. It's "nocent," harmful to the harborer.

In the tercet on "depressive chemicals" I note something that has hit me hard. We're all to some degree controlled by our brain chemistry and body hormones. A person who is felt or thought to have offended you may in fact have been quite miserable while doing whatever it was you didn't like. That's because in bipolar swings or mixtures of mood, sadness can take the form of hostility, or be projected as attack, or come across as enmity.

But if that's true, as to my sorrow I've discovered it often may be, the "offender," so called, isn't guilty and in need of "punishment." Rather, s/he committed the seemingly hostile act or uttered the apparently offensive words when already in a state of at least partial "imprisonment" by the offending chemicals or hormones.

And if you get angry, you then become the next self-punisher. You have to "dree," or endure, the misery you want to inflict. And why want to inflict misery anyway? Love your neighbor, it isn't nearly so life-draining.

Avoiding a "fray" or fight will turn your "gloom" to "glee." The task of punishing an "offender" is one you can't ever "rightly" frame or conceptualize, and for two reasons. (1) You can't get inside the brain, heart, soul of another human. (2) Even if you could, it isn't your job to judge. Instead, look within, and anything needing improvement replace with what is better.

37 Indignant ire is anger all the same

Indignant ire is anger all the same:
We think it justified—yet will it be
Unlovable by one whose mind 'twill claim.

The side effects belatedly I blame,
And small effect of halted ill I see.
Indignant ire is anger all the same.

What guilt I might at first in error name
May rather have awoken nocently,
Unlovable by one whose mind 'twill claim.

Depressive chemicals the mood can maim
Of one deemed foe, who so from guilt is free.
Indignant ire is anger all the same

And feels the arrow it would vainly aim,
The venom that resentment made us dree,
Unlovable by one whose mind 'twill claim.

Pass by the task you cannot rightly frame:
Evaded fray your gloom may turn to glee.
Indignant ire is anger all the same,
Unlovable by one whose mind 'twill claim.

Thoughts on "Of subject-verb the structure's been around"

We have (or, at least, I personally have) a mania for giving structure to things. We're taught in school that every sentence has a subject (the noun—a person, place or thing) and a verb (an action or state of being). We say "The world is," or "John loves Mary." But do we always know other objects' deeds or states of being? Mostly we don't.

That means that most of the sentences we utter are of doubtful truth value. You could say, though, that they express our feelings. Right? Maybe yes, maybe no. Sometimes I utter something that surprises me because it's quoted from an old movie re-run that's been playing in my brain when I was unaware of it. The sentence embodied feelings I had in the past but don't anymore, don't need or even want anymore.

To stop talking for awhile may be a mercy to you and the hearer. It frees you from the tyranny of the sentence, which requires seeming judgments about people and their deeds or states of being—judgments often inaccurate or needless or harmful. Deep breaths can restore awareness, and balance of mind. Deep (silent) breathing also reaches the depth dimension, the space for thinking about what you want your life to be for. You could make a startling discovery about this.

When talking turns to listening, you can hear the music of your life. It may be, as mine will often seem, largely a "canon on a ground bass," a conversation of intertwining themes on a basis of a recurring desire, or a native ability asking to be realized in the world of action, in a state of real becoming.

38 Of subject-verb the structure's been around

Of subject-verb the structure's been around
Awhile. If sometimes neither will appear,
Receive the gift of unawaited sound.

That grace affirmed in breathing may abound,
The will grant rest, and let the seeker hear.
Of subject-verb the structure's been around

To speak of action when direction's found
But needn't make the founding purpose clear.
Receive the gift of unawaited sound.

Our life may shape a canon on a ground
Should mind and heart unite and banish fear.
Of subject-verb the structure's been around,

But let it not the final aim propound.
Strong figured bass might reassure the ear:
Receive the gift of unawaited sound.

A shining star! Your station may astound.
Your searches now converge in higher sphere.
Of subject-verb the structure's been around—
Receive the gift of unawaited sound.

Thoughts on "The underwater mind is ocean-wide"

The Qur'an claims life originated in water, and evolutionary thought has said the same. Our "unconscious" or "underwater mind" is huge, encompassing, dreamlike, and filled with what is living. Says the Lord in Qur'an 21:30, "...we made every living thing of water..."

More: the Unconscious when active in a dream is timeless. It aims for Totality, not recognizing negativity at all, since a Nothing can't be visualized. Things feared are represented as vividly as things wanted, however, and the benefit of *that* is great, for we get to see how our fears and wishes interact, often being compressed together in a single image. These wants and don't-wants can re-appear from any part of our life, and the input from childhood remains powerful throughout our days and nights. When we're immersed in the underworld of our mind, we live a life unbound by clock time. Dream time opens up new space for your past, present, and future to be reimagined by more enveloping and undying elements of your "self."

But the overworld of the sky is equally free of time constraints. Looking at the night sky from the standpoint of what we know about star-life, we realize that the light from any star took millions, billions, or trillions of light years to arrive at the grand occasion for which it was destined: to be met by *your eyes*. The sky spreads out before you a timeless world in which you are immeasurably old while at the same time not losing your present-moment youth. The stellar overworld, like the dreamtime under-one, is filled with living beings, for the stars have lives like our own. The heaven is filled with scattered "presents" from the past.

39 The underwater mind is ocean-wide

The underwater mind is ocean-wide.
I wrote in four-beat lines, then fivers gained
Control that all my conscious will defied.

I didn't hear it—for the brain denied
A strength quite overwhelmingly attained:
The underwater mind is ocean-wide.

I'm droplet mild subjected to the tide
With force that overpoured the dozy-brained—
Control that all my conscious will defied.

I'm bound to heed the waves whereon I ride,
Lest motion from below have weakened, waned:
The underwater mind is ocean-wide.

Two days I wrote in fives—then, weary, sighed:
Oblivion a deeper truth explained,
Control that all my conscious will defied.

Sail on, obedient boat: by rule abide
That fates for you to follow have ordained!
The underwater mind is ocean-wide,
Control that all my conscious will defied.

Thoughts on "How are you feeling now, resistless dream?"

Someone wants to know, "How do you feel at this moment, irresistible dream?" To whom is the question directed?

Here's the broadest interpretation I can think of, and it may be the best. No answer could be simpler. You are the dream.

Ibn Arabi, supreme of Sufi mystic thinkers (1165–1240), taught that God breathed the many worlds into being with a Lover's breath of yearning for something, someone, to love and be loved by. The object of the longing was realized, the dream came true, the wish became reality, because the breath of life that God gave was the breath of His Imagination. We are imagined beings, and our Creator, Whose essence is unknowable directly, can be known in part through His partial reflections in everything He has "created"—which means "imagined."

How do we know the Creator through His imagined creations? By imagining. The plurality of worlds was and is momently dreamt, as we too are, were, and shall be. We, who are dreams, communicate with other dreamt beings by way of our dreaming imagination.

We float along the "sea of Seem," the ocean-flood of appearance, and must be attuned to flowing, as poetry allows. We are a depth which mirrors a stellar height: these two dimensions (which are one in spirit) meet in us, the dreamt, the dreaming.

40 How are you feeling now, resistless dream?

How are you feeling now, resistless dream?
The double nature of the mind's revealed:
Flow on, spry boat, along the sea of Seem.

The heaven, thunder-bold with lightning-gleam,
My under-ocean mirrored, pow'r to wield.
How are you feeling now, resistless dream?

The day of mind must die, that night may deem
Her kinship high to moon and starry field:
Flow on, spry boat, along the sea of Seem.

Two darks will threaten. Him that harks let teem
With hints of when to guide, and when to yield.
How are you feeling now, resistless dream?

I have no thesis, yet can sing a theme:
A soul and starfish float, are never steeled:
Flow on, spry boat, along the sea of Seem.

Then strive, but if you'd thrive be not extreme:
The height and depth let blend, the rift thus
    healed.
How are you feeling now, resistless dream?
Flow on, spry boat, along the sea of Seem.

Thoughts on "A pray'r, disease of will; a creed, of mind?"

To read the essays of Ralph Waldo Emerson (1803–1882), not a systematic philosopher but, like Michel de Montaigne who invented the "essay" (1533–1592) a vigorous thinker, never fails to impart a vigorous joy. "As men's prayers are a disease of the will, so their creeds are a disease of the intellect," claimed Emerson in "Self-Reliance."

Emerson is a poet in prose, and there's one crucial thing I've come to understand about poets: we tell the truths of feeling. Poetry and prose meet in the form of the saying, adage, aphorism, proverb, motto. That's because the abbreviated form compels compression, the density of lyrical concision. You can't expect an aphorism or adage to be true in every context and for all occasions. Often the reverse of a motto is fully as true as the motto. That's why Oscar Wilde and Bernard Shaw found it easy to be witty with proverbs by the simple technique of proclaiming their opposites. For example, Wilde proposed that "Nature follows Art far more than Art imitates Nature" ("The Decay of Lying," 1899). Wilde's motto is poetically true, a metaphor of something deeply felt and important: we see in Nature what we've been taught to see by Art. I'm likelier to find blue and green in snowdrifts than if I'd never seen a picture by Monet.

The truth of an aphorism, then, is a partial truth, and it is a partial truth of feeling. I love the bold saying of Emerson here because I know how he felt every time I've said a prayer merely from supposed obligation, or distorted, fevered hope—every time I've tried to believe something simply because I wanted to. You can't compel yourself to believe things, and there's no point in trying.

41 A pray'r, disease of will; a creed, of mind?

A pray'r, disease of will; a creed, of mind?
So Emerson advised—defiant, he.
Be centered still: petitions leave behind.

Made milder, value and relief here find:
Than mere believer, lover liever be.
A pray'r, disease of will; a creed, of mind?

Breathe deep the air of Being, height-aligned.
Feel undefinable Infinity.
Be centered still: petitions leave behind.

Receive beneath-above as intertwined,
Nor self as tethered, fettered ever see.
A pray'r, disease of will; a creed, of mind?

Imagining's more gladdened and more kind
Than reading of a screed 'mid fallen scree.
Be centered still: petitions leave behind.

Both pray'r and creed containers are, that bind
And shape and color spirit flowing free.
A pray'r, disease of will; a creed, of mind?
Be centered still: petitions leave behind.

Thoughts about "To sing in verse for children evermore"

How did I come to write this? A publisher in Germany commissioned me to translate *Fünf Märlein für Kinder* (*Five Fables for Children*) by poet Friedrich Rückert (1788–1866), a wonderful man who learned 44 languages and translated verses and scriptures from many of them. After completing my delightful task I wrote these glad reflections.

Rückert, who had a total of 20 children and during most of his adult life rarely had fewer than 10 in the house, showed a mentality that appealed to the child in me. His "fables" have no clear moral beyond a jocular imitation of one. He's a joker, and his rhymed verse, in unpredictable patterns of 4, 5, or 6 beats each (or maybe some other number, depending on his mood), will accent the unfettered pleasure of the whimsical childhood imagination.

You'll find violence in the fables, as in all fairy tales. But that's part of the life of every child, who lives in a world made by giants, unaccountably huge beings with irrational demands and personality quirks beyond number.

A tree goes for a walk. Another tree, discontented with the leaves it got, will try out alternative options. A little boy is given free rides by birds and animals. A fiddler makes all the nearby people, creatures, and objects dance, including the castle where he's playing. An elf manages to exit from a goose that had swallowed him.

Rückert wrote elegiac poems that appealed to Gustav Mahler, but he also penned a book of entertaining "domestic" lyrics. One of them tells how to teach your boy to climb a tree.

42 To sing in verse for children evermore

To sing in verse for children evermore
To hear will make the soul belaureled feel,
Refreshed for having opened up a door.

I rendered fables Rückert sang before:
Each melody would limpid rhyme unreel
To sing in verse for children evermore.

The rhythms gave the gliding boat an oar.
The balanced mind is on an even keel,
Refreshed for having opened up a door.

The wing of humor made the spirit soar
That, kindly winking, beckoned the ideal:
To sing in verse for children evermore.

Imagination feels the lure of lore
Enscrolled to send abroad, pure love reveal,
Refreshed for having opened up a door.

Let story poems I for you outpour
Be tender salve and balm, world's hurt to heal,
To sing in verse for children evermore,
Refreshed for having opened up a door.

Thoughts on "Had not the note in thrilliance thralled"

See why I just praised a poet that knows how to appeal to kids? When in a sportive mood, I get as wacky as I like. "Thrilliance" you won't find in any dictionary. "Thralled" isn't a standard word either: I'm using it to mean "enthralled," or captured, captivated. The olden dance called in French a *branle* turned into a "brawl" when the English took it up.

The crazy playfulness won't stop. In my thoughts on poem 42 I evoked the work of Friedrich Rückert, the German counterpart to Dr. Seuss, and he's often in the back, or front, of my mind when the child-time comes to me. Villanelle-writing encourages that: it feels like a game.

As in a music piece that modulates from cheerful major to melancholy or pensive minor, about halfway through you'll note the lyric gets a little more sober with (1) a saying from Solomon's biblical Proverbs and (2) a nightmare nicely survived by the simple means of awaking.

"Better is a dinner of herbs where love is, than a stalled ox and hatred therewith," says the Bible (Prov. 15–17). I added the archaic word "ywis," meaning "certainly." It made for a whimsical rhyme but also a reminder that the King James Bible (Authorized Version) came out in 1611, during the age of Shakespeare, master of colorful vocabulary.

The nightmare "valley" is that "of the shadow of death" (Psalm 23:4), where if I must walk I will "fear no evil."

43 Had not the note in thrilliance thralled

Had not the note in thrilliance thralled
To spread the tone fulfilled of bliss
Where then were hint that heaven called?

To dance the chant, in *branle* embrawled—
How glad enslaved the day by this!
Had not the note in thrilliance thralled

When cry of child in terror bawled,
Were life itself then felt amiss!
Where then were hint that heaven called?

Far better than an ox enstalled
And hate therewith, to eat ywis
(Had not the note in thrilliance thralled)

Love's herb though in a prison walled.
I shaking, waked by shade-form kiss
(Where then were hint that heaven called?),

Walked night-encompassed, unappalled,
Through valley walked, nor feared abyss:
Had not the note in thrilliance thralled
Where then were hint that heaven called?

Thoughts on "A revelation of transcendent things"

The "magian" or wise man I mention in the second tercet is my Sufi mentor Ibn Arabi, who in *Meccan Openings* declares that an infinite intellect, such as a universe creator must have and apply, will allow no devoted soul to "rest in peace." God never discloses Himself (or Her- or Itself—pronouns, like all words, are only metaphors) except in the most rapid flashes, and no two disclosures are ever alike, so no beholder will ever experience two identical revelations.

Religion, to a poet like me, must be an energizer, not a tranquilizer. We are meant to be pilgrims, Ibn Arabi claims, who travel to ever higher stations, who "journey on from plane to plane" (Qur'an 84:19). Every god, creed, ritual, or prayer is a cup or glass, a container giving shape and color to the water of spirit. Beliefs are knots, capable of tying things together, but also of tying you down—or up.

Muhammad is said to have ridden the steed-like creature Buraq ("Lightning") when transported from Mecca to Jerusalem. In shaman rituals, the enchanter's drum is transfigured into a horse which he will ride to defeat the inner demons whose cries he duplicates while acting out the purifying drama he composes, performs, and undergoes.

Everything is intertwined with everything else, the transcendent (what "climbs beyond") with the immanent (what "remains within"). The seeker alert to the nanosecond quickness of revelation can feel the spring in winter, the winter in spring, epiphanies conveying the breadth of Infinity to us, the seemingly bounded beings. We are never quick enough to keep up with God.

44 A revelation of transcendent things

A revelation of transcendent things—
One flash a nanosecond overflow—
Wealth unencompassed to the bounded brings.

Two moments are too long, the magian sings,
For one disclosure—far, oh far too slow
A revelation of transcendent things.

We're finite-minded, if potential kings,
Nor ever comprehend what, high in low,
Wealth unencompassed to the bounded brings.

The steed of Love he rode that challenge flings:
Who 'rest in peace'—oh, bad!—can barely know
A revelation of transcendent things.

Apollo, Torah, Cross, Qur'an are wings:
The goal unknowable to which we go
Wealth unencompassed to the bounded brings.

All winters hold the seed of many springs,
And summers make the flames of autumn glow:
A revelation of transcendent things
Wealth unencompassed to the bounded brings.

Thoughts on "For me who am alive the duty stands"

In thoughts on poem 31 I introduced the Sufi theory of Names, the paradoxical idea that the Divine Potentials are not only Names that are called but Names that do the calling. The summoner can be any of the potentials, attributes of Total Being, any of the Names that could become your own.

I realized at age 59 that I could be named Poetical Translator, and at age 61 that my newer name would indicate the related station of Original Poet. The word "honey-tongued" evokes the metaphor that ancient Greeks fashioned to describe a verbal singer's gift. It embodies the musical impulse to create a harmony, a sweetness to charm the ear.

The free winds of heaven are mentors to the poet, who wants to rival them in force and gusto, to feel their timeless freshness that goes beyond "yore" (the past) and "yon" (spatial distance).

Originality means your source is the Origin. All branded objects, ready-mades, are slave-brands. They subjugate through the wiles of the great tempter, Trend. Every poet is both Homer and Odysseus when chanting his own odyssey of exploration. Defying the lure of the crowd, he'll watch for the wandering cloud.

The lucky mariner will be led, following poet Arion, to the locale of his oracular calling by a dolphin, or guardian spirit. The Delphic oracle was the one to which Arion had been guided by a dolphin, emblem of a fertile and flexible intelligence.

45 For me who am alive the duty stands

For me who am alive the duty stands,
However great were they who've long since gone:
Take action when the summoner commands.

Let serve the minstrel-work with active hands
The honey-tongued that gods had called at dawn:
For me who am alive the duty stands.

Love thrusting wind that captain-lung expands
To rival, to surpass the yore and yon:
Take action when the summoner commands.

The branded object subjugates. It brands,
It brags, "The high will thrive, so bow and fawn!"
For me who am alive the duty stands

To guide the craft to unawaited lands,
To chant the valor-deeds that bear me on:
Take action when the summoner commands.

Prepare today to sail from barren strands.
Find oracle, be led by dolphin spawn.
For me who am alive the duty stands:
Take action when the summoner commands.

Thoughts on "To Essence call an opening your Guest"

Every opening to a unique momentary disclosure of the Unknown to our metaphoric Imagination is like the coming of the angels to Abraham, the affable, welcoming host to whom they will bear miraculous news of the forthcoming birth of a son in his and his wife's old age.

Every angel is a uniquely appropriate bearer of a personally directed disclosure. That's merely a symbolic way of saying that each of us has the capacity to receive a type of epiphany that differs from anyone else's.

That is the guiding assumption of my investigations gathered in *Patterns of Epiphany* (1997) and elsewhere. I look for recurrent patterns in the collected revelations of a major imaginer. Often these are manifested most completely in what I can call a "paradigm" epiphany where the disclosures hinted at throughout the seer's work are unfolded in full glory.

I can give a recent example. In *Victorian Literary Cultures: Studies in Textual Subversion* (ed. Kenneth Womack and James M. Decker, 2016) I wrote "Moonrise and the Ascent of Eve, the Woman-Titan: Charlotte Brontë's Epiphanies of the Fourfold Elemental Feminine." Here the paradigm is found in the novel *Shirley,* where we're granted the heroine's vision of Eve as Mother of the Titans (including Prometheus and Oceanus, or fire and water), the spirit of Nature at worship (air and earth) invoking Genius, at once her god and her own creative powers—a giant, a striver with Omnipotence, begetter of Messiah, "well-spring of the blood of nations" and uniter of the elements of our world. She reappears thrice in *Jane Eyre.*

46 To Essence call an opening your Guest

To Essence call an opening your Guest.
Why momently of shifting shape? 'Twill need
A change, for wakeful mind-play cannot rest.

For you is revelation manifest
Of such a kind as no one else can heed:
To Essence call an opening your Guest.

From what one seër finds to be the best
Revealer, others' view-range will recede:
A change, for wakeful mind-play cannot rest.

The self, one moment past, had effervesced.
Another came and left, with heaven-speed.
To Essence call an opening your Guest.

Revealer and perceiver share the quest:
Imagining of souls to love must feed
A change, for wakeful mind-play cannot rest.

In thinking, dreaming, we'll the holiest
Of efforts make, that metaphor be freed:
To Essence call an opening your Guest,
A change, for wakeful mind-play cannot rest.

Thoughts on "To read in horoscope and see in sky"

Why not picture your fate acted out in the heavens by mythic gods? To abandon astrology and horoscopy is a bit like whitewashing the allegories of saints' lives in the churches, the way William Shakespeare's alderman father John was deputed to do. You have less to imagine. Even if Buddha's focus on personal self-conquest through meditation was designed to supersede the mythic systems of the Hindus, the same epic-dramatic impulse can be found revived with splendor in the detailed Indonesian sculptures of Borobudur. And although the gods and all their colored realms depicted in monastic mandala paintings are scattered into the component sand grains once the elaborate symbolic patterns are produced, just as the envisioned deities themselves are transpierced and banished by the Buddha, a single glance of whose eye could dispel ten thousand demons, nonetheless the art-drive urging the monks to make their disposable masterworks ought to be accounted a major testimony of our undaunted love for imaginative beauty.

Born on the second night of Passover, as a boy I liked picturing myself as having two birthdays and two identities. My lunar-calendar Jewish birthday moved around freely in the springtime while my solar-secular birthday remained unmoved at April 21. However, even the seemingly unchanging latter day had its double identity. It's often the first day of Taurus the bull following Aries the ram, so I might be pictured on a "cusp." And that's imaginatively arousing because Taurus acts bull-headed in defense of the status quo while Aries can be called the vernal innovator. Maybe that will help explain why I want to be the kind of pioneer who discovers things so old they had been forgotten, despiséd, rejected, or banished.

47 To read in horoscope and see in sky

To read in horoscope and see in sky
And dream of lunar phases' light and shade
Will give you range, the low become the high.

'Twill gently tell, best comrade standing by,
What rest and movement altered map have made
To read in horoscope and see in sky.

If planet placement, mood of star-group nigh
Arouse or mirror dark, the pattern-braid
Will give you range, the low become the high.

The spectral tone, that counsel would supply,
The kind advisor, calm, will offer aid
To read in horoscope and see in sky.

Your psyche newly iatrized and sly
Feels liberated that the game well played
Will give you range, the low become the high.

As Jove approaches Virgo, Taurus, why
To task of Saturn tired attention paid?
To read in horoscope and see in sky
Will give you range, the low become the high.

Thoughts on "Coordinate each deep-drawn breath of air"

I love rocking chairs and use one at intervals throughout the day. The cradling movement, maybe dating back even to the awareness, within the womb, of Mother breathing in and out, contributes to what a psychologist might call creative regression. The pleasure is so immediate and compelling that I risk unwanted comedy if I begin the rocking while holding a coffee cup that might readily overspill—and that has happened.

I care about tidal motions with an intensity one may find unusual. The to-and-fro movement relates to the inhaling-exhaling of our breath. I have even compared breathing to begetting, with their ins and outs.

We only rose gradually out of the ocean and are still mainly composed of water, so we're tidally inclined from start to finish.

The crescent-moon curvature of the rocker-runners hybridizes chair and wheel to let you sit and travel at once. For years I loved rocking my daughter to sleep. Sitting while moving puts me to sleep if I don't take coffee or tea, and when I'm on a car ride I barely stifle yawns. I've been told that babies can be pacified with a brief car trip: often they will fall asleep quickly and easily.

I don't fear regressive infantility, for a sound sleep is needed if you want to draw on the dream world when you sing your lyrics later. Ernst Kris defined artistic creativity as "regression in the service of the ego."

48 Coordinate each deep-drawn breath of air

Coordinate each deep-drawn breath of air,
While watching cup-borne coffee rise and fall,
With back-then-forward movement of the chair.

A tidal mindful universe you there
Will find, as by the waters' quiet call,
Coordinate each deep-drawn breath of air.

A child on breast of mother resting fair
Must know in throat, heart, lung the tide of All
With back-then-forward movement of the chair.

Our breathings rocking body movements bear
Of cradled creatures wrapt in water-shawl:
Coordinate each deep-drawn breath of air.

While floats in plenilune the molten flare,
One feels the moon-might heft on large and
    small
With back-then-forward movement of the chair.

Pray blend with mine, dear Friend, your silent
    pray'r
Of thanks that we in depth can, heaven-tall,
Coordinate each deep-drawn breath of air
With back-then-forward movement of the chair.

Thoughts on "You've noticed in my float-sway reverie"

Notably presented as key to the meaning of the entire novel *War and Peace* as well as of history and individual human life (Tolstoy was always ambitious), a dream of pendular motion such as I depict in my rocking-chair reveries turns out to be the paradigm epiphany of Tolstoy the Visionary.

In Pierre's dream, a schoolteacher points to a classroom earth-globe and explains that historical movements, like the western advance of Jenghiz Khan and the eastern one of Napoleon, are pendular like the tides in the ocean. He further tells that the individual soul is a water-drop rising to life and then subsiding into oneness with that ocean.

In an essay about Tolstoy's great historical novel, Isaiah Berlin quotes Greek poet Archilocus: "The fox knows many things, but the hedgehog knows just one thing." Tolstoy, in Berlin's view, was a fox who wanted to become a hedgehog. And the hedgehog aspect of *War and Peace*, the unifying vision at which the author wants everything to converge, is the dream I just described.

Tolstoy lost his mother at an early age and wrote a counteractive idyll that he called *Childhood,* an idealizing portrayal of those early years, meant to lessen the trauma. The pendular salvific reverie, too, may be an idealizing, compensatory maternal, tidal, oceanic, and spirit-cradling epiphany.

Napoleon, for this Russian author, is a droplet on a crested wave. Naturally he'll soon fall. He was not the moving current but the object moved, the bubble burst.

49 You've noticed in my float-sway reverie

You've noticed in my float-sway reverie
Two motions, poet-praised, would coincide:
Front-back the chair, in-out the breath of me.

In *War and Peace* the dreamer thought there'd be
The movements twain, that ever would abide,
You've noticed in my float-sway reverie.

East, west, on sweep and swing of history
Napoleon or Jenghiz Khan would ride:
Front-back the chair, in-out the breath of me.

Each bubble-soul would rise from out the sea
To live, then die and in the deep subside
You've noticed in my float-sway reverie.

The east-west tide, the up-down motion we
Could find in bliss that childhood can provide:
Front-back the chair, in-out the breath of me.

Tallstory, you discourse quite lengthily
Upon a memory for which you sighed:
You've noticed in my float-sway reverie
Front-back the chair, in-out the breath of me.

Thoughts on "If you envision an epiphany"

Here I'm indulging the pleasure of recounting a few discoveries I made in my *Patterns of Epiphany* already cited. Writing that book made me feel like a scientist. Every time I'd uncover the paradigm of a recurrent epiphany pattern of element-movement-and-shape, I'd feel like leaping for joy: the formula had been found!

But there's yet a greater, deeper joy that comes from the overarching, underlying thought that both grounds and animates the book. A principle of value emerges. It would appear that every major imaginer (maybe every human being?) has the gift of receiving-creating a unique epiphany pattern that can affect us all in parallel ways when we read it in a book, but that affects the imaginer of the pattern with special, induplicable, irreplaceable intensity.

To make a literary epiphany requires two gifts: receptivity and formative power. You feel the epiphany as something that comes to you, a revelation, yet at the same time you craft and fashion it in your work of literary art. You are analogous to a dreamer who had a revelatory visitation at night but who must reshape it by daylight, perhaps in an Augustinian "confession" or a kabbalistic parable or a Franciscan hymn.

The uniqueness of the element-movement-shape pattern you create lets you offer a contribution to the total human treasury of epiphanic experience that no one else could ever have made. I am transfixed and exalted by this thought.

50 If you envision an epiphany

If you envision an epiphany,
And should thereafter it revisit you,
You'll element-shape-movement pattern see.

An awe-filled dawn-rose and a wheel would be
What Tennyson would glimpse, what you might
    view
If you envision an epiphany.

Red-yellow fire-bloom, white bird's death, pardee,
You, Walter-Pater-like, indeed might rue:
You'll element-shape-movement pattern see.

To fire the stones might turn, bright, lightning-
    free,
As when by Barrett Browning's eye pierced
    through,
If you envision an epiphany.

Frail shapes may shiver, tremble feveredly
And they for Coleridge aye were wont to do:
You'll element-shape-movement pattern see.

Eruptive fires the hero-minds would dree
When following, Carlylean, their cue:
If you envision an epiphany
You'll element-shape-movement pattern see.

Thoughts on "My freedom will its rival not have bested"

The ridiculous can be sublime if the key to wholeness, holiness, turns out to be "adjestment." As anger may lead one to madness and vanity, good humor's the secret of gladness and sanity. An old-time college drinking song went like this:

> Gaudeamus igitur
> > Iuvenes dum sumus!
> Post iucundam iuventutem.
> Post molestam senectutem,
> > Nos habebit humus.

> Let us keep rejoicing then
> > While we yet are young!
> After passing gladsome youth,
> After age and pain, forsooth,
> > Into dust we're flung.

I offered "dust" for the harmony with "flung," but of course the Latin says "humus," which every gardener knows about.

Witty adjestment frees you from contention with competitors. All poets are friendly rivals: "anxiety of influence" can be considered as big a danger to mental health as anxiety of theft by progeny would be. Art is game-like, playful. Imagination, in the form of boy-god Hermes, may be viewed as light-hearted, even prankish. Inventor of the poetic lyre, he leads us to the next world or state of being.

51 My freedom will its rival not have bested

My freedom will its rival not have bested
Though strive it might to conquer stronger fate:
To ardent heart let head be well adjested.

Should every aim stay mainly unmolested,
Calm compromise you may congratulate:
My freedom will its rival not have bested.

Capacity by challenge rightly tested,
Advancing is enhancing: never wait.
To ardent heart let head be well adjested.

Our human humus humor's life-invested,
That change we, welcoming, might celebrate:
My freedom will its rival not have bested,

Yet if I write, not merely having rested,
Mellifluent the lyric I'll create:
To ardent heart let head be well adjested.

'Tis requisite for pilgrim to have quested
Attempting to attain a high estate.
My freedom will its rival not have bested:
To ardent heart let head be well adjested.

Thoughts on "The marvel of the writing life unmarred"

In Milton's *Paradise Lost* we learn of the difficulty of the "dark descent," from which the poet strove "to re-ascend, / Though hard and rare" (III.20–21), words derived in turn from Vergil's *Aeneid* VI:126–131. Milton's own misfortune involved blindness, and his re-ascent from the trauma was in part achieved by the poetic shaping of that victory in the lines I quoted from.

In this seventeenth-century pre-Romantic passage Milton is becoming his own poetic hero, as Wordsworth would be later in his verse autobiography *The Prelude.* Such poets combine the roles of Homer (poet, author, "minstrel") and Odysseus (epic hero). Like the hero, they descend to the underworld (as Milton traveled to Hell in *Paradise Lost*), then re-ascend from the pit, as Milton's therapy for blindness was to rise to a level where he could view and depict "things invisible to mortal sight" (*PL* III.55).

The re-ascent is "hard and rare"! Even the work itself, once written, is in peril. So in a Dead Sea scroll we read David's "Psalm 151," as it has been called, a poem that fell into oblivion for two thousand years before re-discovery. I remember the thrill of reading it in an Israeli museum.

Dying god legends like those of Christ and Mithra require a fall and rise. Vergil sang about "arms and the man"—the struggle of Trojan Aeneas to rise from Troy's defeat and go on to found Rome—while Milton sang of Adam and Eve, and later (in *Paradise Regained*) of Jesus. But all poets chant their own marvel of a writing life, creating a work perdurable to outlast our mortal span.

52 The marvel of the writing life unmarred

The marvel of the writing life unmarred
I sing, not arms with Vergil, nor indeed—
To urge the worth of lyric rise, though hard—

Mere clever wit of deft Ulysses, barred
From song (for that, a minstrel he would need).
The marvel of the writing life unmarred

I praise. An agéd parchment-remnant charred
We prize if it be perfect prophet-screed.
To urge the worth of lyric rise, though hard,

A chant I raise, I treasure tablet shard
Whereon a psalm of David we may read.
The marvel of the writing life unmarred

I lift to heaven. Let the soul have sparred
In struggle. Ev'n defeated, mind 'twill lead
To urge the worth of lyric rise, though hard.

Who follow light, their guide is northern-starred.
Exulting is exalting. Hearken, heed
The marvel of the writing life unmarred
To urge the worth of lyric rise, though hard.

Thoughts on "No star's outvoted in the lighted sky"

The friendly rivalry of kindred souls will likely always be a favorite theme of mine. When I translated Johann Wolfgang von Goethe's *West–East Divan* I wrote my "commentary" in verse. It was a set of poems even more numerous than, though correlating with, Goethe's originals. That's how I showed I wasn't imitating (copying) the German poet but emulating (rivaling) him. And I was only doing what Goethe himself had done, as announced in the title of his poetry "collection" (the meaning of the Persian word *divan*). "West-East" meant that while Goethe was learning from his "eastern" mentor, the medieval Persian pub poet whom in the poem "Unbounded" he called his twin brother ("we twins have grown"), he was still retaining his "western" identity as a modern German poet.

Rivalry, friendly emulation! I love it. And it starts within. The true, deep, original meaning of the word *jihad* in Islamic moral theology is the struggle between the higher and lower selves, a struggle central to all three Abrahamic religions: Judaism, Christianity, and Islam. You can think of your life as a race of the two selves, to see which will soonest attain the goal of God's favor. That's why I've written, "Our dearest rival is the one most nigh, / The lesser I, that may 'gainst higher jar."

To "deem" is to judge, aver, assert, affirm. Our lives are imaginative constructions that we make through our choices, and from that standpoint we're all dreamers, all our deemings are dreamings. A *ricercar* (pronounced ree-chair-car) is a richly complicated musical fugue.

53 No star's outvoted in the lighted sky

No star's outvoted in the lighted sky
For right to life by one deemed brighter far:
All deemers dream. What's vital is to vie.

Implicit challenge—that is vying. Why?
Mere envy's hate, but love will gates unbar.
No star's outvoted in the lighted sky.

To vie is to invite: our aim is high,
For height is depth where central values are.
All deemers dream. What's vital is to vie.

Our dearest rival is the one most nigh,
The lesser I, that may 'gainst higher jar.
No star's outvoted in the lighted sky:

The secret sharer, not to be put by,
We'll integrate, to shape a *ricercar.*
All deemers dream. What's vital is to vie.

Come, heaven-breath, we'll cowards quite belie:
Seed fertile make in worldwide seminar!
No star's outvoted in the lighted sky,
All deemers dream. What's vital is to vie.

Thoughts on "Devotion is reliant on a vow"

Two main ideas—one at the poem's beginning, the other at the end—are rivals here, and that is their tensile strength.

The opening sentence offers a thought that issues naturally from just looking at a word and studying the history of it. "Devotion" comes from the Latin word *votum,* meaning a vow (or by extension prayer, votive offering, wish, longing). When you're devoted to a goal, you promise or vow to yourself that your work will stay focused until it is achieved.

The final quatrain compares the would-be devoted person to a tree, an organic unity of harmoniously interacting components where the whole is more than the sum of the parts. It also explains what makes the tree viable for growth: it has an "entelechy," Aristotle's word for a growth principle. This Greek philosopher of self-actualizing liked to say, "The acorn loves to become the oak." The inner principle of growth dictates your development and the meaning of your life insofar as that meaning is evolved through your self-realization in thought and deed.

Devotion is based on keeping a promise made. Entelechial guidance is based on heeding your growth-principle as guide. Devotion means you've selected a goal to pursue. Entelechial growth means your development from "acorn" to "oak" is largely unconscious: "The root, the bole [= trunk], the leaf, and eke [=also] the bough" interact in ways beyond conscious planning. But willed devotion and unconscious growth may combine if you think of your growth as height-directed and try to "rise," as the tree will.

54 Devotion is reliant on a vow

Devotion is reliant on a vow.
We hope to bring creative strength to light,
Day-creatures lending life: the future's now.

Though time's aflow, afloat, we anyhow
Becoming may with Being make more bright:
Devotion is reliant on a vow

A structure to erect that yet may bow
To fluxile thrust with humble mirror-sight,
Day-creatures lending life: the future's now.

The day's a thing you make if we allow
That times are shapen as with music-might:
Devotion is reliant on a vow.

I only ask that Power me endow
With patience that may guide my will aright,
Day-creatures lending life: the future's now.

The root, the bole, the leaf, and eke the bough
Am I in You, entelechy of height!
Devotion is reliant on a vow:
Day-creatures lending life, the future's now.

Thoughts on "For circle-world each look's an upward ray"

People's tendency to compartmentalize experience can have tragic or entertaining results. We tend to think of a religious "heaven" in the sky because this bit of early childhood instruction gets walled off from what we later learn about a Newtonic universe where up and down are quite arbitrary notions. You'll find no up or down in the world of astrophysics.

A helpful imaginative remedy to this walling off is the exercise of trying to picture people standing on a globe, where rightside up and upside down lose meaning. They don't exist for actual people: we all look "up," or so we feel and, in practical terms, think. You can "rise" from wherever you are, for rising is a condition of imagination, of spirit, of envisioning, not of literal direction.

So you can't tell by looking whether you or someone else climbs "up" or not. But we're always changing, becoming, moving. The planet itself travels: "pilgrim," or religious traveler, and "peregrine," or avian sky-traveler, are in this regard no different from planet Earth and the solar system and the galaxy. We're all headed somewhere, but the up-ness or lack of it is for you to imagine.

Compartmentalizing is active in the preserving of childhood simplicities in the "adult" mind. Heaven, earth, and hell remain the three stories of a department, or rather compartment store. Compartmentalizing may give us a god who creates 100 billion galaxies, each with unimaginably many stars in it, and who then carries on a coupling with a submicrobially tiny creature on a crumb of rock.

55 For circle-world each look's an upward ray

From circle-world each look's an upward ray
As from a radiant and rounded sun:
We height attain wherever we might stay.

Do trend and creed and cower-crowd affray
Your will? If timid, life had ne'er begun.
From circle-world each look's an upward ray.

Our planet is a traveler. Our way
Is pilgrim-peregrine, no journey done:
We height attain wherever we might stay.

Embrave me, modern *chant de geste* or *lai:*
Who'll judge if hero lost, or if he won?
From circle-world each look's an upward ray.

My spheric eye and whorlèd ear yet may
Give impulse, help me hymn the course we run:
We height attain wherever we might stay.

With voice and violin I'll sing and play
Hid wonders that if glimpsed the mind would stun.
From circle-world each look's an upward ray,
We height attain wherever we might stay.

Thoughts on "Where vigor's matched with rigor would I dwell"

Mevlevi (or Maulana) Shemseddin Rumi, Persian-born though he lived for decades in Turkey (1207–1273), may be the supreme mystic poet both for quality and quantity of inspired verse. I've translated 99 poetic selections from a German rendering of his work, in a book soon forthcoming.

My favorite German rendering of Rumi selections keeps the verse form he loved best, the *bait*, a rhymed couplet with two six-beat lines, analogous to the hexameter or alexandrine couplet in European verse. Rumi wrote many thousands of these. Modern translators in English have most often ignored the form along with eliminating Islamic and Qur'anic references. Formally of an extreme intricacy and deeply, richly learnéd in their content, Rumi's poems can't be accurately heard when these two qualities—of form and content—are passed over as inessential. They mattered to him, and they matter to me. "Twin-rhymed, near-hexametrical the spell"—that's the body of the spirit.

To match vigor with rigor motivates me to write villanelles in much the way it motivated Rumi to write his myriads of mystical couplets. The sensation of writing Rumiesque twinned verses in English makes the renderer feel exultant, exalted, "enstelled" (raised to stellar height).

To be the comrade, the friend, of a poet means to love the forms that the kindred spirit loved. And—with Rumi—what a spirit! He "wed the fire with sky and heavened hell"—he likened the world to a giant fire whirling about the Presence of God. In the Qur'an fire is most often a punishment, but in Rumi, founder of the Whirling Dervishes, we are all energies in the world's flaming dance.

56 Where vigor's matched with rigor would I dwell

Where vigor's matched with rigor would I dwell.
The dance of energies by Rumi made:
Twin-rhymed near-hexametrical the spell.

He wed the fire with sky and heavened hell.
He in a headlong heartstrong fervor swayed.
Where vigor's matched with rigor would I dwell.

O comrade, friend, of you I gladly tell
Who fear of being strange can bold evade:
Twin-rhymed near-hexametrical the spell.

Who tides can feel may drink from spirit-well.
I've danced with you in thought, with you have
    prayed:
Where vigor's matched with rigor would I dwell.

My voice to utter joy will psalm impel.
Be word-created light in tone arrayed!
Twin-rhymed near-hexametrical the spell.

Me rhythmic verser may a verve enstell:
Beat, rhyme I'll serve till I'm in coffin laid.
Where vigor's matched with rigor would I dwell,
Twin-rhymed near-hexametrical the spell.

Thoughts on "A triumph in the battle that you wage"

I interpret "liberal education" as the kind that liberates you from the trap of the trendy present and its randomly imposed regime. Physically we live at a particular time in history, but in spirit we can travel past that point, beyond incarceration in the mode that people think has been decreed.

World navigators can choose their mentors from a space unbounded, an unstipulated time. Bridge building starts from the realm of the person whose culture you're visiting. You translate poems or scriptures or scriptural poems from that person as situated in his/her culture, and then, in replying through poems incorporating the lyric forms you've just been taught through your apprentice work, you connect the place (physical, cultural, spiritual) that you've been visiting to your ostensible "home."

"Lazy clay" turns to Rumiesque fire under the stimulus of what your chosen mentors have achieved.

57 A triumph in the battle that you wage

A triumph in the battle that you wage
Against the lazy clay of lethargy
May let you aid the folk of future age,

Defying what some trend-proclaiming sage
Might make a spirit-aim for you and me.
A triumph in the battle that you wage,

Resisting, though with patient calm not rage,
A plan that as inadequate you see,
May let you aid the folk of future age.

The disenfranchised can their pain assuage:
To learn what brothers love will surely be
A triumph in the battle that you wage.

World-circumnavigator is the mage:
Who kindly friend can find beyond the sea
May let you aid the folk of future age.

Each day is blank till we have writ the page.
To love the rigor that one chose will free.
A triumph in the battle that you wage
May let you aid the folk of future age.

Thoughts on "The dead are blessed who at night return"

Being a night person makes it the most natural thing for me to imagine any of my never-dying mentor-choices coming back from the realm of stillness to visit me.

All the great singers may be likened to the Sons of God who in the Book of Job chanted glory at the dawn of the creation. They have not stopped but must be heard, as the seraphs, each a burning angel, must be viewed, by those intent upon writing the scripture they would themselves most love to embody.

"By seed on high enspermed no life I spurn": this means we are all equally the god-begotten who want, each, to be a voice of the grateful world.

The sober visitants tell of mercy inevitable as the morning dew.

Including every gender-merit or virtue, from *vir* (Latin for "man") as from *virgo* (Latin for "young woman") and from *virga* (Latin for "staff, twig, walking stick"), all filled with *vires* (Latin for "energies, forces"), the night-come guardian I seek has the form of woman, man, or child.

The evening star is the morning star and both are Venus (Roman) or Aphrodite (Greek), a variant of whose name is our "April," the month when I was born. My birthday, the 21st, comes at the juncture point of Aries the innovator and Taurus the defender of established value.

58 The dead are blessed who at night return

The dead are blessèd who at night return:
They entryway most readily attain,
For 'tis from these I lasting lore may learn.

I for the yonder than mere yon must yearn:
Come therefore, living sprites, re-dawn my brain:
The dead are blessed who at night return,

That heart more pure with seraph-ray might
    burn.
My urge to fame they purge—oh, major gain,
For 'tis from these I lasting lore may learn.

By seed on high enspermed no life I spurn:
Nonmanifest, the depth we can't explain.
The dead are blessed who at night return

With face that may be earnest yet not stern
And mercy tell of first and latter rain,
For 'tis from these I lasting lore may learn.

A smile I glad descry and light discern
Of shining star to guide on ocean main:
The dead are blessed who at night return,
For 'tis from these I lasting lore may learn.

Thoughts on "What happened to the people made like me"

These words have the lamenting burden (a word that means not only a load to bear but a refrain to hear) of a verser to whom a prosy world means the fate of a Philomela, the silenced nightingale. Waiting for Beckett's Godot (God as O, the Big Zero) seems equivalent to a state of a-musement or no-muse, Poesia Abscondita, poetry as hidden goddess.

But that isn't my mood today. People have been coming to my Nikolay Gumilev YouTube to hear poetry declaimed, dramatically acted, in the old style.

I've been trying to imagine what a 19th century "elocution" course would be like. This training was ubiquitous in America: learning how to recite musically-written poems, dramatic monologues, acting scripts in lyric form, in a way that lets the meaning be apprehended and the rhythms and tone-harmonies at the same time be savored.

I'd love to attend such a class. The technique is a subtle one. You have to keep two things in mind at once, and always. The dramatic feeling and the accompanying plans, thoughts, contemplations, hopes, regrets have to come across. And their force of emotion must be full-strength too, so "natural" speech or prose conversation-talk is not appropriate at all. Rather, some syllables will be just the tiniest bit lengthened, others correspondingly shortened, to make up the poetical rhythm performance.

E-locution means projected speech, talk that reveals where it comes from.

59 What happened to the people made like me

What happened to the people made like me,
Word harmonies who crave, and metric feet?
They couldn't all have died—where did they flee?

Shakespearean, Miltonic poesy,
And Chaucer's, Dylan Thomas', had a beat.
What happened to the people made like me?

Vast lunar dunes might landscape seem to be:
I wait for gone Godot, a-musement sweet.
They couldn't all have died—where did they flee,

The sonnet bards with love-tone artistry?
Brave balladeers whom Schubert *Lieder* greet?
What happened to the people made like me?

Come, holy Roman Horace, hear my plea!
Bring classic meter, to the ear most meet!
They couldn't all have died—where did they flee,

My kindred singers? Crying dolor dree
The philomels prepared for winding-sheet.
What happened to the people made like me?
They couldn't all have died—where did they flee?

Thoughts on "We Shakespeare call immortal, but he's dead"

> Hark, hark! The lark at heav'n's gate sings,
>   And Phoebus 'gins arise,
> His steeds to water at those springs
>   Of chaliced flow'rs that lies,
> And weeping mary-buds begin
>   To ope their golden eyes.
> With everything that pretty is,
>   My lady sweet, arise!

I'm suggesting the larks in this tune from *Cymbeline* no longer sing to waken sun-god Phoebus, to open the eyes of marigolds, or to awake a lady. Songbirds vanish when plays are performed with no regard to the music. Here, in *The Tempest*, Prospero complains about an attempt to overturn his rule:

> This King of Naples, being an enemy
> To me inveterate, hearkens my brother's suit;
> Which was, that he, in lieu o' th' premises [= in exchange
>   for the guarantees]
> Of homage, and I know not how much tribute,
> Should presently exTIRpate me and mine
> Out of the dukedom and confer fair MILan,
> With all the honors, on my brother. (II.ii.120-127)

The 5-beat rhythms are annihilated unless we pronounce the problem words the way I indicated. Shakespeare often said things differently than we do now.

60 We Shakespeare call immortal, but he's dead.

We Shakespeare call immortal, but he's dead.
No mary-buds their golden eyes will ope:
No lark is Phoebus waking, sleepyhead.

Iambic lines—no longer sung but said.
Words twisted, mispronounced—abandon hope!
We Shakespeare call immortal, but he's dead.

Deaf ears don't hear what reader-eyes have read.
Deaf editors will hand you hanging-rope:
No lark is Phoebus waking, sleepyhead.

I spoke of meter, and away they sped,
Who, troubadour-contemners, toneless grope:
We Shakespeare call immortal, but he's dead.

With scansion-bliss unknown, we'll tell instead
Of chanting in a dream on meadow-slope—
No lark is Phoebus waking, sleepyhead.

Eight centuries' pure forms to death are wed?
Then, best of friends, to heaven let's elope!
We Shakespeare call immortal, but he's dead:
No lark is Phoebus waking, sleepyhead.

Thoughts on "When I have died and you, my friend, shall see"

A oneness-thinker, I can't imagine a severed soul, but rather the idea of a matter-energy, a body-like spirit. What factor, being, or deed can "miracle" a person's matter-energy? What makes it a thing of wonder?

In tercet 1, the body's chemicals and hormones are the miracle makers for the integrated living unit and union.

In tercets 2 and 3, the poet's friend can miracle his own body-spirit through the realization that the poet's legacy lives on in him when he writes.

In tercets 4 and 5 I admit I've been talking about myself and my friend. I claim to have achieved a measure of freedom by embracing the Name, the Being-potential, that summoned me, the mission of poetic singer. Even fuller, deeper liberation, I then claim, will come when my friend understands what I've said and done regarding the Name and thereby gives it new life. The legacy of that embodied Name becomes an "interfact," a link of two body-spirits.

In the final quatrain it is my friend who now miracles the matter-energy that I had and was, and that I wanted to transmit and give in friendship. My friend understands, more fully than ever, that inner and outer, living singer and dead one, living soul and surrounding cosmos, are interrelated in a shared joy, emblemized by the invigorating breeze (wind-spirit, bearing nourishing heaven-dew to earth) that enlivens the grass which has lain devoutly prostrate in morning prayer.

61 When I have died and you, my friend, shall see

When I have died and you, my friend, shall see
The collocated chemicals are gone
That miracled this matter-energy,

Pray institute a dialogue with me:
A resurrection comes with every dawn.
When I have died and you, my friend, shall see

From heart now turned toward eternity
New art may rise, the path you'll travel on
That miracled this matter-energy.

When rightly claimed, my Name had come to be
A sign, the gliding freedom of a swan.
When I have died and you, my friend, shall see

That, through your eyes alive, I spirit free,
To shape an interfact may strength be drawn
That miracled this matter-energy.

The inner and the outer interspree.
The breeze will yet refresh the prostrate lawn
When I have died and you, my friend, shall see,
That miracled this matter-energy.

Thoughts on "The root of 'random'—*run*; the 'chance' root—*fall*"

Here's one of my favorite kinds of poem to write: a root inspection. "Random" and "chance" are words that appear to make mishaps inevitable. But their roots relate the two to many kindred phenomena—disappointing, heartening, or both at once. Each error that we make in a world of random chance is an indication of life: it is the price and reward of action. We achieve by trial *and error.* We try things out, we take a chance, we run a risk.

The word "random," in its origin, relates to the word "run." It's a motion word, like "err," whose root has not only the meaning of making a mistake but also that of wandering. A "knight errant" wanders while he looks for deeds of knightly valor that need doing. He may wander "aberrantly" and be thought to have gone astray, but that's hard to prejudge.

Chance is a kind of falling, as with the fall of dice, which may foretell what "befalls" you, whether of good or ill. Unfortunate "accidents" are root-related to "chance," but it's often suitable, as well, to speak of a "happy accident." Another kindred word, "occasion," is appropriately neutral. Germany's greatest poet J. W. von Goethe claimed that all his poems were "occasional," meaning he went through life trying to make the most of any occasion, whatever might befall. "Cadence" is a beautiful relative of the fall-words, for a cadence is often a harmonious and gratifying resolution, as at the conclusion of a piece of music.

Another fall-word, one of the best, is "casual." With a casual approach to random chance, the aberrations of the knight errant, despite the risks run, prove occasions for a pleasant cadence.

62 The root of "random"—*run*; the "chance" root—*fall*

The root of "random"—*run;* the "chance" root—*fall.*
One views the word when picturing a deed.
Each error's life-sign: let it not appall.

Mistakes would fain escape, they're often small—
But even "accident" my strength can feed.
The root of "random"—*run;* the "chance" root—*fall.*

"Occasion," "cadence," "accident" recall:
In random "chance" a favor I should heed.
Each error's life-sign: let it not appall.

Occasion cadenced—grace of crystal ball.
The cited words bear wisdom I will need:
The root of "random"—*run;* the "chance" root—*fall.*

Found objects may the dreaming mind enthrall:
Though "accidental," these for art-use plead.
Each error's life-sign: let it not appall.

Knights errant err. Aberrant? No, not all.
Run random? Happy happenstance! Godspeed!
The root of "random"—*run;* the "chance" root—*fall.*
Each error's life-sign: let it not appall.

Thoughts on "*Sub*—up to; *limen*—limit, threshold, sill"

Seeking the "sublime," we're ready to go the limit. I wrote this poem to remind myself that the word is not merely a category of art theorizing or classification, it's an objective depiction of what science did for me personally.

Today those of us lucky enough to get checkups and medicines can live twice as long as our grandparents did. The five medicines I list (and perhaps more to come) keep me alive with a disease that disabled at age 53 my spiritual-musical grandfather, Charles Ives (1874–1954).

This man changed my views of what musical structure might entail. His *Sonata No. 2* for violin and piano (which I play on violin with pianist Asher Raboy on martinbidney.com) creates composite beauties of a kind I would have thought impossible, including reels, jigs, ragtime, hymns, and time signatures altering with every bar.

But diabetes grabbed him at a time when cures weren't available, and his composing career was cut short—though not till after his four symphonies, chamber works, and perfect songs ranging from whimsy to the highest height had come into being for our lasting pleasure.

In the eighteenth century Age of Enlightenment it seems to have been obligatory for every poet to pay verse tribute to Sir Isaac Newton. To the scientists who have given me a poetical life that began with translations at age 59 and with original poems at age 61, I hope my blog-and-poem will serve as tribute.

63 *Sub*—up to; *limen*—limit, threshold, sill

Sub—up to; *limen*—limit, threshold, sill.
The word a promised land expands for me:
Sublime—we grapple high, with eager will.

The forecast brain with terror-dream may fill:
Wild storm for some indeed might mortal be.
Sub—up to; *limen*—limit, threshold, sill.

All lives are short—each one must Fortune kill.
To urge more breath, more breadth—blest
    energy!
Sublime—we grapple high, with eager will.

I thunder seem to hear, though heav'n be still.
A roar, a shout: let heartbeat sound more free!
Sub—up to; *limen*—limit, threshold, sill.

Metformin, zocor, and lisinopril,
Tradjenta and omeprazole agree:
Sublime—we grapple high, with eager will.

With lyric tonic, scientific pill,
I help the harking soul to hear and see.
Sub—up to; *limen*—limit, threshold, sill:
Sublime—we grapple high, with eager will.

Thoughts on "Spread wealth. The unaware can't ask for alms"

In this poem my sources are Jewish, Islamic, Hellenic, and Hindu.

In the Qur'an 47:38 we read, "And as for him who hoardeth, he hoardeth only from his soul." If you hide things away, you hide them from yourself. We should be generous, shedding our sunlight on all. We should open opportunities to those who don't yet know that these exist: One of the 5 pillars of Islam is the giving of alms.

The 17th century musical instruments whose wealth of beauty I recommend sharing are those I heard dialoguing over my head as a youngster. I'd go to hear a brass concert, and the brass choir on stage would converse with the one in the balcony.

Two wonderful psalms tell of the need to share, not hoard. Psalm 42:1 says, "As the hart panteth after the water brooks, so panteth my soul after thee, O God." The young deer gets the water needed for sustenance and for survival.

Psalm 92 says, "12. The righteous shall flourish like the palm tree: he shall grow like a cedar in Lebanon. 13. Those that be planted in the house of our Lord shall flourish in the courts of our God." Generosity received in the realm of the holy reveals its rootedness in the heart.

Bassarids and corybants worship gods of fertility (Dionysus and Cybele).

The inner and the outer, world and spirit, are one in A-U-M. "A" opens you up to World. "U" directs you inward to Spirit. "M" dissolves the boundary.

64 Spread wealth. The unaware can't ask for alms

Spread wealth. The unaware can't ask for alms.
In writers "blocked," blest energy you'll plant:
Inhaling songful pow'r the spirit calms.

In words, play tabret, sackbut, trumpet, shawms.
Hear deep in quiet. Be the hierophant.
Spend wealth. The unaware can't ask for alms.

Light scatter: they'll be nourished by your
    psalms.
Hymn waterbrook whereafter harts will pant.
Inhaling songful pow'r the spirit calms.

In courtyard of the Lord the upright palms
Feel yet in eld the flowing sap, not scant.
Spend wealth. The unaware can't ask for alms.

I fearless hear, belying timid qualms,
Frenetic bassarid and corybant:
Inhaling songful pow'r the spirit calms.

Nondualism is the tune of AUMs.
The Yígdal is a dancing anthem-chant.
Spend wealth. The unaware can't ask for alms.
Inhaling songful pow'r the spirit calms.

Thoughts on "In growing old I readily forget"

It's very straightforward, yet there's a question, too. What are the "two more identities" that "awake" in tercet 5? Why the apparent total of 4 identities?

Again I play the role of root inspector. What is the root meaning of "ecstasy"? The word has two parts: *ek* + *histanai*. The *ek-* means "out of, out from." The *histanai* means "to place, to cause to stand," related to *stasis* or "standing."

When you're in ecstasy, you're "beside yourself." You feel as if there were "another you," with a changed nature, standing next to you. The word embodies a vivid image of being "born again," but with concurrent awareness of your higher and lower identities or natures.

Getting older, I forget the thousands of poems I have translated and written. They come to me as embodying other selves. Each newly re-discovered poem I find brings back the "ec-stasy" I was in while writing and after the writing was done. I remember not only the flight, the height, but also something of the "daily me" that I was at the time of writing. These are the two novel, or newly re-felt, identities that suddenly come.

Every remembered ecstasy, then, is the remembrance of a twofold state when you were "beside yourself." This, in turn, can bring on a corresponding condition in the present moment, the moment of remembering. Total = 4 identities.

65 In growing old I readily forget

In growing old I readily forget
What I have done and felt, conceived and writ.
And is there benefit in this? You bet!

May whiskaway of past impression let
Old work resurface new, refreshed, re-lit.
In growing old I readily forget

What days of yore have shown me—and reset
Imagination-gauge, new times to fit.
And is there benefit in this? You bet!

A lyric when I'm favored to beget,
Beside-myself, ec-static am I smit.
In growing old I readily forget

How I'd been moved. Yet, frenzy now re-met,
Two more identities awake from it.
And is there benefit in this? You bet!

We're child-like once again, my friend—a debt
That Time has granted—gift I cheered admit.
In growing old I readily forget—
And is there benefit in this? You bet!

Thoughts on "'Tween poem and psychosis, I contend"

A friend makes the difference between writing poetry and going crazy. The psychotic may live through experiences of astonishing poetic depth, yet lives them in a world that seems to belong to the sufferer alone. Also, writing a poem may give you the feeling you're writing better than you could possibly deserve, better than you had ever dreamt would be possible, and at that point you may feel as if you might burst from happiness. What a relief, what a rescue, to be able to tell someone about it! Either a sad or a happy madness can be helpfully confided to, and sometimes healthily moderated by, a friend. The "guardians" helping to distinguish writing from raving are you and your friend.

The comrade may be one who loves you personally (tercet 3) or may be a poetic rival or fellow-writer, with whom a degree of tension may be a stimulant (tercet 4). We're all pilgrims, wandering seekers, and in tercet 5 I suggest that the difference between our good and bad fortune as we both progress and go astray might be the friendships we maintain.

Our "angel-name" is the mission, role, purpose, goal, and provisional identity we choose in responding to what feels like a summons, a "calling." To realize our potential in this chosen vocation means making choices continually. The perspective of a friend will help.

I write a poem every day (or more than one, or more than ten—whatever I choose) and send them to friends, always.

66 'Tween poem and psychosis, I contend

'Tween poem and psychosis, I contend—
And every day I live proclaims it true—
The difference may be defined: a friend.

Of happiness that never has to end
Or lead to madness, guardians are two
'Tween poem and psychosis, I contend.

Entrust your love to one who will commend
Devoted faithfulness, nor soul eschew.
The difference may be defined: a friend.

Should comrade be a rival and contend
In emulation, rift you still won't rue
'Tween poem and psychosis, I contend.

Us pilgrims, wheresoever we may wend,
With fortune good or bad will life endue.
The difference may be defined: a friend.

To earn our angel-name that fate may lend,
Contrasted things we'll see, distinct our view.
'Tween poem and psychosis, I contend,
The difference may be defined: a friend.

Thoughts on "To be a friend and daily offer aid"

Our correspondence never ends, even though we only write to each other once or twice a year. I'm reluctant to name him, for he's modest. Earlier employed as a teacher, he has high credentials in Persian music and Sufi mystic writings. But he quit that line of work in favor of daily service in a hospice for the dying.

He plays music for them when it is wanted. He reminds me of American poet Walt Whitman, who during the Civil War comforted many a dying fighter in the hospital, and who has written poems about this. Whitman's "When lilacs last in the dooryard bloomed," a funeral elegy for Abraham Lincoln, draws on many years of helping people by thoughtfully sharing their fate.

To say that my friend's hospice work "[m]ust be a gift by heaven-depth repaid" means that a spiritual depth will be inevitably gained by devoting one's days to friendship.

Depth and height are the same in the world of spirit. In Sufi thinking, we rise, in our pilgrimage, to ever higher "stations" or levels of awareness.

Whenever he writes me, he mails a translation of a Persian poem or saying, embodying new awareness or betokening the hope of it.

Like Whitman (still America's favorite poet), my friend is a teacher of Oneness, a comrade of the dying, and a blessing to me.

67 To be a friend and daily offer aid

To be a friend and daily offer aid
In hospital to those that wait to die
Must be a gift by heaven-depth repaid.

I know a man who this a mission made.
He, listening, stays comfortingly nigh
To be a friend and daily offer aid.

A Persian zither likely he'll have played.
Kind conversation, with a smile or sigh,
Must be a gift by heaven-depth repaid.

Walt Whitman blessed each fighter, unafraid
To kiss the wounded at their last good-bye,
To be a friend and daily offer aid.

By angel grace that selfish will outweighed
Our lifelong inner conflict to defy
Must be a gift by heaven-depth repaid.

Dear Friend, your Sufi zither is arrayed
For me, today, in light from gentle eye.
To be a friend and daily offer aid
Must be a gift by heaven-depth repaid.

Thoughts on "A clever way to complicate the mode"

This poem is playful and practical, too. I play around for awhile with images of writing: experimenting with new phrasings made possible by new bowing techniques (I'm a violinist, and fiddler), or thinking of ways to keep the rowboat smoothly moving, propelled by the "turning current."

Then, starting with tercet 4, I consider practical ways of varying the interest of the writing to add appeal. Look at the phrase "oar in able hand": it's compact and packs a punch, offering a quick movie-closeup of the rower. But the "nominative absolute" phrase is syntactically (structurally) connected only in a loose and floating way with the rest of the sentence. This construction is something I first learned about in Latin class, where it was called an "ablative absolute." Julius Caesar, in our high school version of his *Gallic Wars*, often began a sentence with "Which things being so" (*Quae cum ita sint*). In English class we later got appealing examples from the teacher. "Gun in hand, the killer stalked his prey." "The sun setting in the western sky, we bade farewell to the friendly isle of Ubi-Ubi."

"Volitive subjunctive" is the construction where you express a wish: we're saying, "Let [or: may] such and such happen!" "Be the load more weighty!" "Long live the king!" [short for "Let the king live long!"]. "[May] God forbid!" This, too, can be quick and vigorous, another punch-packer.

More tricks: "Play long-and-short." Use "subject, verb made canorous [= singable]" when they're aligned but when the "and" is omitted from "subject [and] verb."

68 A clever way to complicate the mode

A clever way to complicate the mode
Of writing villanelles to jolt the mind
Repays the greater effort then bestowed.

The trick is limber syntax: fiddle bowed
To vary phrasing type, I know you'll find
A clever way to complicate the mode.

A boat along the turning current rowed
To keep the driving impulse right behind
Repays the greater effort then bestowed.

With nominative absolute, you showed
That, oar in able hand, you had designed
A clever way to complicate the mode.

With volitive subjunctive, be the load
More weighty than deemed bearable! The bind
Repays the greater effort then bestowed.

Play long-and-short. A fragment. Dead-end road.
Or subject, verb made canorous aligned:
A clever way to complicate the mode
Repays the greater effort then bestowed.

Thoughts on "With crisp attack in clicking touch of keys"

Here I write—with sensual pleasure—about the sensual pleasure of writing.

The clicking of computer keys brings to mind the intensely pleasurable music of E. Power Biggs, who used to play baroque organs or authentic modern copies, with an incisive, slightly percussive beginning, or "attack," to each of the tones.

More recently, the late lamented Jonathan Biggers, Professor of Music at Binghamton University, used to conclude each of his Bach recitals with precisely the jig-fugue that I remember most vividly from many childhood hearings of Biggs performing it. Typing on my accordion-like computer keyboard (an ergonomic one with split halves connected at the NE corner of the left square to the NW corner of the right one) makes me feel like these musicians, patron spirits of all who love typing as a purely physical action.

And nothing more than the simple thought of writing as bodily pleasure will bring back repeatedly another bliss: writing high school plane geometry theorem proofs on lined white paper with a Sheaffer cartridge fountain pen. I loved the bright blue ink, and it was a wonder to see the moist traces dry before they could smudge. What a gift to a left-handed boy who couldn't write with a no. 2 pencil without producing a page of dreary gray!

In my poem this memory in turn leads to phone conversations I used to have with a schoolboy friend who lived up the block. He would help me solve the theorems, and I would help him construe the Latin in our high school edited version of Caesar's *Gallic Wars*. We learned much this way. We learned friendship.

69 With crisp attack in clicking touch of keys

With crisp attack in clicking touch of keys
E. Power Biggs made organ jig-fugue leap.
Thus you, computer keyboard, speak of ease.

Distinctness and precision fingers please:
The playful line finality may keep
With crisp attack in clicking touch of keys.

Yet letters flee: the tender streamlet breeze
Lends gentler pleasure to the brisker sweep:
Thus you, computer keyboard, speak of ease.

Blue ink, my schoolboy pen, the memories!
The pleasure in calligraphy went deep.
With crisp attack in clicking touch of kcys

I add to flow more potent expertise.
My Euclid proofs in blue I won't beweep ...
Thus you, computer keyboard, speak of ease.

We traded aid—math, Latin. Harmonies
Of student friendship, lasting, never sleep!
With crisp attack in clicking touch of keys
Thus you, computer keyboard, speak of ease.

Thoughts on "Muhammad likened milk to knowledge high"

The Qur'an is largely a book of biblical stories about Jews and Christians: we learn little of the prophet himself, though what we do learn shows him to be a lovable though fallible being. I particularly treasure sura (chapter) 80, called "'He Frowned,'" where the Prophet is chided for having conferred with an influential rich man while a blind seeker of aid was slighted. As the teacher learns from his own negative example, he grows in stature before our eyes, and we, in turn, are learning.

Since we hear so little about Muhammad from the Qur'an, we turn to the hadith or memoir literature to read the exhilarating narrative accounts written by disciples and relatives. We envision the three angels that visited Muhammad on a mountaintop, where they excised his heart to remove a speck of impurity and then replaced it, soothed by cooling liquid. We're told of his trip from Mecca to Jerusalem on the back of a horse-like animal called Buraq or Lightning, and of his tour of the heavens and meetings with the prophets. And we come to know of Muhammad's loss, at birth, of his father and later, at age 7, of his mother.

The Prophet never forgot his loving debt to his foster mother, who raised him. In the hadith literature we hear him say, "Paradise is beneath the feet of the mothers."

I think his fondness for the metaphor of milk as representing the nourishing pleasure of knowledge may relate, deeply and intensely, to Muhammad's love for his foster mother. In yet another hadith he expresses thanks for three of life's greatest wonders: Fragrance, Woman, and Prayer.

70 Muhammad likened milk to knowledge high

Muhammad likened milk to knowledge high:
When shines the white on pure computer screen
You see the sun at height in noontime sky.

"New doctrine will be granted by and by,
Hid wisdom shall in heart be heard and seen."
Muhammad likened milk to knowledge high...

Who spoke the cited words? The deepest "I,"
That rose from tired old man to child pristine:
You see the sun at height in noontime sky.

Serve Wisdom well, be wise, computer spry!
Her field is Eden, She the holy Queen.
Muhammad likened milk to knowledge high—

Maternal nourishment that none deny—
And none may blessèd Mother-love demean.
You see the sun at height in noontime sky

Whose light will worry and concern belie:
The welcomed liquid light is kind, serene.
Muhammad likened milk to knowledge high:
You see the sun at height in noontime sky.

Thoughts on "False Falstaff, Hammy Hamlet, shall I say?"

Humor is a potent method of survival. In poem 51 line 10 I even picture the human as the meeting point of humus and humor.

So when I've read or viewed and heard too many news reports, I take to whimsied versing for refreshment and relief.

In this peculiar fancy, I note that two qualities of two respective Shakespeare characters may be thought to combine in a presidential candidate who shows a liking for drama. The sullenness of Hamlet, without his depth of conscience, and the loose mouth and living of Falstaff, without his engaging wit—the less central, less valued qualities of the two characters are oddly appropriated, and distorted in a cartoonish way, by the person in question.

The villanelle may be judged little more than a cartoon. But I need humor: it has been my habit for years to read the comics in the daily papers before I look at the headlines. It even became a joke in my parents' house: when I'd ask, "Would you please pass the international news?" my sister understood that I was asking for the comics page in the evening paper, pleasingly named *The Daily Herald-Telephone*.

My natural inclination in verse-writing is not to comment on politics, and even here the thoughts are a bit oblique, fitting the elusive topic. Yet as a professor of political science pointed out to me lately, "You may not care about politics, but politics cares about you."

71 False Falstaff, Hammy Hamlet, shall I say?

False Falstaff, hammy Hamlet, shall I say?—
Are intertwisted in our politics
In quite an odd, unprecedented way.

A loose-mouth clown and woman-hater may
Combine and raise a crisis—how to fix?
False Falstaff, hammy Hamlet, shall I say?—

Opportunistic followers today
Repent misguided presidential picks
In quite an odd, unprecedented way.

Odd method, that of wayward fortune-sway:
No "god from the machine" cries "nay" or "nix."
False Falstaff, hammy Hamlet, shall I say?—

We ask: why such a long-drawn Shakespair play
To witness till our strange impression sticks
In quite an odd, unprecedented way?

Fake bluster may the fools, not fates, affray
Though Emperors Unclothed have many tricks.
False Falstaff, hammy Hamlet, shall I say?—
In quite an odd, unprecedented way.

Thoughts on "Of bards to whom we most attached have grown"

The gift bestowed on a "gifted" person might be better called a loan. You pay it forward.

The love that Muhammad received in the legend where he was allowed to touch the Heaven-throne with his sandal was a gift that his followers repay when they hang up in their homes a sandal plaque with calligraphic writings telling what the story has meant for them.

The way a poet repays the loan is by writing a poem, or a book of poems, or a lifetime of them.

The water miraculously gushing up from stone, as happened for Moses during the wandering in the desert, may be likened to the sudden rising from the Unconscious of a gleam from the depth of the Unmanifest.

The miserable love company perhaps even more when the "company" is one who sings to them what they had wanted music-drive to utter. Ralph Waldo Emerson thought we were all poets. That is why in "Self-Reliance" (1841) he wrote, "In every work of genius we recognize our own rejected thoughts; they come back to us with a certain alienated majesty." The alienation that gave distance to the majesty may have come from the feeling that we had too soon discarded what would have taken more faith to shape as art. But there is a majesty to the comfort offered by chanter, angel, friend. It is the grandeur of the universality of woe and joy.

72 Of bards to whom we most attached have grown

Of bards to whom we most attached have grown
We like to claim they have a special gift:
They're favored with what I would name a loan.

The Prophet-sandal touched the Heaven-throne.
He shared the love so given, hearts to lift
Of bards to whom we most attached have grown.

If we are grateful, may the will be known
Which healers body forth who seal a rift:
They're favored with what I would name a loan.

A fountain verse we make to burst from stone
To add our strength to effort slow or swift
Of bards to whom we most attached have grown.

The music that was moved by lovers' moan
Made hearts rejoice of wanters balked or miffed:
They're favored with what I would name a loan.

Be you my Friend, who know the lure of tone!
Be lulled by summer melody adrift
Of bards to whom we most attached have grown:
They're favored with what I would name a loan.

Thoughts on "Of many-voicéd ocean Homer sings"

"Momently" means "every moment," as "daily" means "every day." If a thing is momentary, it lasts only a moment, and if a thing is done momentarily, it is done only for a moment. To hear on a telephone that someone will be "with you momentarily" means the person will be with you only for a moment, and that is not reassuring at all. Why do people who work in offices keep saying "momentarily" when they really mean "in a moment"? Is the long word more official-sounding?

Exploring our nature "momently" would be quite a project! It would mean nonstop self-scrutiny. The discipline of unrelenting mindfulness, difficult and maybe only viable for brief periods of concentration, is commensurately rewarding, though. One reason I've been writing a daily villanelle is to concentrate, while I'm doing it, on minute details of thinking, feeling, rhythming, rhyming, phrasing, and intoning.

The commentary (by Rabbi Adin Steinsaltz) to a mindfulness-guide called *Tanya* (by Shneur Zalman of Liady) distinguishes between struggle with God and struggle *in* God. In the same way, we can be mindful both as a swimmer distinct from Ocean and as a water drop that is part of it. The ocean sung (praised in verse) by poet Homer is "in the self abiding"—it is in him, as the Ocean is in the water drop.

Also, the gadfly to which the philosopher Socrates compared himself is a drive, an impulse, a compulsion to achieve a meaningful kind of motion in the Shoreless. Maybe poetry will help me view Ocean by lending "wings" to fly above it, for some moments, in the music of its thought.

73 Of many-voicèd ocean Homer sings:

Of many-voicèd ocean Homer sings:
Our nature if we momently explore
We learn what may be known from journeyings.

Polyphony of tone the motion brings:
What billions of potentials we ignore!
Of many-voicèd ocean Homer sings

That, in the self abiding, challenge flings:
Drives choiring in the mind the tones outpour.
We learn what may be known from journeyings

Who heed the gadfly that, Socratic, stings
And swim to buried treasures' living lore.
Of many-voicèd ocean Homer sings—

And one who, scion of the island kings,
Would sail and shove aside the homeland shore:
We learn what may be known from journeyings.

The writer's fingers are the mindful wings
That fly where first the soul had rowed with oar.
Of many-voicèd ocean Homer sings:
We learn what may be known from journeyings.

Thoughts on "The female sprite that chanted e-mailed lines"

Ecclesiastes 11:1. "Cast thy bread upon the waters, for thou shalt find it after many days." A metaphor of a gift made for its own sake without hope of reward shows that rewards unexpectedly come from the attitude behind the gift.

Writing songful villanelles, you're doing what the proverb recommended. You write each line in hope that more will come your way. Unquestioning, you write what comes to you, shaping it into something the hands like to make and the brain to calculate, the heart to feel and the inner ear to listen to.

You can watch the winds on the lake when you throw the bread chunks, for wind and water currents as they interweave suggest the half-aware creativeness which is unpredictably shaping what you're chancily producing.

To do these things and enjoy them, you only need faith in your ability to do them, faith in what you are, not by your merits but by your nature. We're made to create. That's why we imagine creator gods, to model what we value most. We also make deities who are women, who bear children. There are hundreds of these wide-hipped figurines from 'round the globe, hinting strongly that the oldest impulse in our god-making drive was to offer images of birth. Craft will always involve birth and will be intertwined with it. Sex may be passion but love is an art.

Sending a child out from the maternal body into the world, or from parental protection to adult independence, is like the casting of bread upon the waters.

Maeve is better known as Queen Mab, meaning in Gaelic "She who intoxicates."

74 The female sprite that chanted e-mailed lines

The female sprite that chanted e-mailed lines
Commanded, "Cast your bread upon the wave:
You'll find it later, as your fate designs."

"I hear a silence that my wit confines:
How, from the quiet, singing word to save?"
The female sprite that chanted e-mailed lines,

Replying to the query, kind, divines:
"Believing what I claimed, you'll be more brave.
You'll find it later, as your fate designs."

"I'll, grateful, Lady, try to heed the signs
That lie within the winds that surface lave."
The female sprite that chanted e-mailed lines

Replied: "I'll not prescribe you anodynes.
It isn't gone, what breath on current drave:
You'll find it later, as your fate designs."

Right understanding never undermines
The drunken-making tune of Irish Maeve,
The female sprite that chanted e-mailed lines:
You'll find it later, as your fate designs.

Thoughts on "Should I, upon awaking, try to say"

Rather than the guidance that the structure of a villanelle, with refrains presumably worth repeating, would seem to encourage, here my frequent returns to the same theme are more like the hesitations of the nervous beginner wondering about recurrent questions hard to answer.

Maybe you can guess from lines 12–14 that what bothers me is American politics in its more dire potential, as viewed today. I'm dejected.

Curiously and hearteningly, there's a tradition of exploring "dejection" in English poetry. Coleridge wrote "Dejection: An Ode" (1802). Shelley composed "Stanzas Written in Dejection, near Naples" (1818), Keats an "Ode on Melancholy" (1819). Causes for depression range from Coleridge's frustration with his laudanum addiction (and misguided attempt to project the blame onto his caregiver) to Keats' more philosophical treatment of melancholy as part of the transitory nature of things, though the poet was likely impelled also by the syphilis, tuberculosis, and mercury poisoning that would combine to kill him in his 26th year.

My worry in this poem is far lesser, even trivial-seeming, since I'm only wondering how my poetic arts and crafts can have any effect in a tragic national situation, while it is the national problem that more deeply concerns me.

"Can grace our fate from cataclysm spare?" At least my question isn't foolish. It is central. And my hopes are as deep as they are continually underwhelmed.

75 Should I, upon awaking, try to say

Should I, upon awaking, try to say
A thing so keen, concise that it would bear
A thesis where the structure yet might stray

Athwart the page and there provide display
Of what with proverb wisdom-wit might square?
Should I, upon awaking, try to say

What connoisseurs of wryness may find fey—
Firm world-concern in statement free of care,
A thesis where the structure yet might stray,

Attempting to distinguish "let us pray"
From "let us prey" where kindness may be rare?
Should I, upon awaking, try to say

What use debating if an insult slay
Deep, reasoned discourse and befoul the air?
A thesis where the structure yet might stray?

'Twere best to try to keep my fears at bay...
Can grace our fate from cataclysm spare?
Should I, upon awaking, try to say
A thesis where the structure yet might stray?

Thoughts on "Converse in iamb and pentameter"

I'd hardly be surprised if people said,
"You've gone bananas, bonkers, 'round the bend...
That plan you're hawking—strictly looney tunes!"

Calm down, my friends, and try it out, all right?
What topic would you like for starters, huh?
The weather's good ... Do February days
That feel like springtime mean we'll pay a price
In March that no one's even dreamt of yet?
And oh, those eagles floating in the air—
How wonderful to spot them coming back—
They nearly went extinct in New York State!
Of course I grant they like to gather where
Some folks are raising chickens ... Heard the news?
The bus fare's cheap for Canada from here.
Ha ha. But—wait a minute—did you see
The EPAC play? Six women took the stage
And talked—amazing what they talked about—
Failed marriages, failed kidney—sadness, jokes—
Lousiana ladies' hair salon—
That's where they were, and Weezy—she's the grump—
Made cracks you hoped you never would forget!
The play? Oh, *Steel Magnolias.* Tell me, friend,
You think we're starting a pentame*trend*?

76 Converse in iamb and pentameter

Converse in iamb and pentameter—
Let's try it, friend, as in a Shakespeare play!
Great game: who could decline? The mind's awhir.

Hymn Queen Elizabeth! All praise to her,
Diana, Ariana, dryad, fay—
Converse in iamb and pentameter:

I'll write the kind of sonnet she'll prefer.
Proclaim Elizabethan Holiday!
Great game: who could decline? The mind's awhir.

We'll speak in meter! Sure, you can demur—
Speak prose unless you'd boldly cry, "Hurray!
Converse in iamb and pentameter!"

Participants might make a sign: "We spur
Past time to reawake, as versing may!"
Great game: who could decline? The mind's awhir.

Sweet William, come alive! We can aver:
The music that you made, youth's heart will
    sway.
Converse in iamb and pentameter!
Great game: who could decline? The mind's awhir.

Thoughts on "The dog that shepherded the waves that sped to shore"

Cervantes' Don Quixote hypnotized himself. He, the simple Alonso Quixano, came to believe that he was really the noble "Don Quixote" because he believed in his altered name. He believed the windmills he was fighting were knightly foes. In the form of a peasant woman he saw Dulcinea del Toboso, a perfect aristocratic lady for a knight of his imaginative standing, her identity as fictive as his own.

The dog shepherding the waves at the San Franciso Half Moon Bay (I had forgotten the name when I wrote the poem) I call quixotic, for he too had been self-hypnotized into an identity that wouldn't leave him.

The running dog and the knight errant are intense imaginers, each an example, delightful and pathetic, of our general dilemma and response. We're all poets and can hardly help it. Religions create hero gods or god-men who are shepherds gathering their flocks, with the aid of many an earthly "pastor," the Latin word for "shepherd." As for the Babylonians Marduk (his name echoed in "Mordecai" from the Book of Esther) conquered Tiamat, the power of darkness, likewise the deity of the Abrahamic religions defeats Devil or Satan. The Christian man-god even gathers up his sheep with the added goal of keeping them separate from goats. A she-goat, like a woman, has no season of "heat" but can be interested in passion all the year 'round, and any potential of lustiness unbridled is deemed a peril.

Moral judgments alter with time, but the poetic, self-hypnotic drive remains. We turn it to a game or sport, while at the same time contemplating the ideal we need.

77 The dog that shepherded the waves that sped to shore

The dog that shepherded the waves that sped to
    shore,
Who seemed to carry out a task which had to fail,
To poet gave a present that a lesson bore.

The San Francisco bay—its name I ken no more
But never will forget, so long as loves avail,
The dog that shepherded the waves that sped to
    shore.

If they behaved the way they'd always done before,
Yet faithful guide, in miming a quixotic tale,
To poet gave a present that a lesson bore.

He got to know the waters, ev'n their whims adore,
By gathering them home within their rightful pale,
The dog that shepherded the waves that sped to shore.

Such unrelenting exercise can health restore
In runner and in watcher, too: a comrade hale
To poet gave a present that a lesson bore.

Then is the guarding act a fiction? Poet lore
Would say: So's every art or sport, for boon or bale.
The dog that shepherded the waves that sped to
    shore
To poet gave a present that a lesson bore.

Thoughts on "When Rumi vision-rapt in whirl of song cried out"

A poet's imagining of Oneness might bear the temptation of lulling "one" to sleep. The pre-Socratic thinker Parmenides of Elea (born about 515 BCE) may have been a mystic dreamer of this kind, for he pictured spherical Being as entirely at rest—all motion, he contended, was illusory. We have to smile at this, the way the Eleatic paradox-makers likely smiled when they proposed "proofs" of the deceptiveness of all movement. I remember laughing, in my schoolboy days, when I learned that Achilles could never catch the tortoise who had a head start in the race. Before Achilles could reach the point where the tortoise was, he would first have to cover half that distance. But before he could cover half that distance, he'd have to cover half of that half. And before … You can finish the puzzle yourself: it's clear he'll never reach the tortoise. I'm told that only calculus can solve the problem …

Yet Mevlana Shemseddin Rumi's vision of Oneness will never present such a stumbling block. It's filled with life—with the lives of all of us. We are the bundles of flaming energy that constitute the whirling circle of creation, dancing around its loving Maker. All is not pleasant in the Round Dance. When God asked the future beings in their pre-created forms within His mind whether they would accept the responsibility, the "Trust," of supervising His works, they all refused save the future Adam or Mankind. He said "yes" (Qur'an 7:172), but the Persian word for "yes," if the accent is just a bit shifted, means "affliction." The affirmation of responsibility will entail the endurance of affliction. So the dance is in large part an energetic struggle. Poets will love to hear this: our art is a struggle, our struggle an art. And Rumi (1207–1273) might be the greatest mystic poet who ever lived.

78 When Rumi vision-rapt in whirl of song cried out

When Rumi vision-rapt in whirl of song cried out
As if bestirred by olden Zoroaster-fire
He poured the molten ore in lines that silent shout.

He proved the truth he spoke by what he told about:
We learned we're each a *zarra*, atom of desire.
When Rumi vision-rapt in whirl of song cried out

His face like Moses' shone, admitting of no doubt:
"We're all a cosmic dance and universal choir!"
He poured the molten ore in lines that silent shout,

"Our ancient trust and godly mission never flout:
God asked if we to be His regents would aspire!"
When Rumi vision-rapt in whirl of song cried out

He added: "Glad, we answered, Yes! But pride don't tout:
Though *bála*'s 'yes,' *balá*'s 'affliction.' Harder! Higher!"
He poured the molten ore in lines that silent shout,

"We strive and we advance. The lower 'I' we rout.
We chant, and dance, and love the Lord, and never tire."
When Rumi vision-rapt in whirl of song cried out
He poured the molten ore in lines that silent shout.

Thoughts on "A lyric diary will map the road"

The two opening tercets give you the words that show where I'm "coming from." These words are "horizon," "pilgrim," "sowed," and "essayed."

First, horizon. Here's our human situation as outlined by philosopher Edmund Husserl (1859–1938). There's a consciousness. And that consciousness confronts a world. A world is something with a horizon, and a horizon keeps changing. These four common-sense ideas are the starting point for what Husserl called "phenomenology," or the study of appearances, analyzing how our world appears to us while we live in it, and live it. To me, the starting point is itself an entire philosophy, and it fits my own sense of being and becoming.

I'm an awareness of a world that has a horizon changing every nanosecond. This makes me a pilgrim (the second of my orienting ideas), a seeker who wanders, a wanderer who seeks. As a pilgrim in the form of a poet, I make a journey in my lyrical journal. Experiencing a world means feeling every day how your horizon changes. In folksong club I used to sing the gospel hymn beginning "I am a pilgrim and a stranger." In Sufi study I encounter the idea that we are all ascending through stages or "stations" of awareness. If we all "live and learn," we're all pilgrims.

"Light is sown for the righteous, and joy for the upright in heart," said the psalmer (97:11). Concept three is the sowing of light, the planting of a potential for insight or wisdom, that the journeyman's journal may offer. We try things out, we "essay" them. That, finally, is what Michel de Montaigne (1533–1592) meant when he invented the modern word "essay" to describe each entry in his life-writing project.

79 A lyric diary will map the road

A lyric diary will map the road
The pilgrim trod that soul-horizon sought
And show the finder who a light had sowed,

Essayed to paint, assayed the day in ode
That, aided by the tuneful muse, he wrought.
A lyric diary will map the road

That glad he'd travel, prodded by the goad
Of rivalry with lower self in thought,
And show the finder who a light had sowed.

What he had learned observing, lightsome load
To bear in bliss, he thankfully had taught.
A lyric diary will map the road

With borders hermed where sudden moment
   glowed:
He'd chant what azure-blue illumined brought
And show the finder who a light had sowed.

He'd often smile, deciphering a code
That the Unmanifest in part had caught.
A lyric diary will map the road
And show the finder who a light had sowed.

Thoughts on "*Repent* is linked to pain, *regret* to weep"

"Gently label them, and then move on." I put the words in quotes because they might be a line of poetry: they came to me this way. And I left them like that because experience may prove how hard it is to speak by any other means than word music about the chief idea imbibed from the many essays I've read by Pema Chödrön, the skilled and cogent Buddhist expositor. The idea is to banish repentance, regret, remorse in favor of a gentle touch, a dispassionate and tranquil labeling, of anything that happens.

A thought, impulse, feeling, or act is something that happens. By quietly, softly naming it, by describing and placing it in a context of other happenings, you arrive at an understanding of it, and then you can move on. The main point and purpose will be always to move on, so you can live more, not less. Worrying about what has happened prevents more and better things from happening.

To "dwell on" something you'd rather move away from means you still "live" in that something. You're stuck there. To steep a past moment in a brine of corrosive examination and self-condemnation is to brew bitterness. Tears are the salty brine in the keg.

Every belief or creed, every religion or poem, is a container for the water of the human spirit, giving it color and shape. But containers mean an end to movement, so to move forward—and that's what animals of all kinds are meant and designed to do—means putting a label on the container. What's contained is in part something that happened, and you want more, better things to happen.

80 *Repent* is linked to pain, *regret* to weep

Repent is linked to pain, *regret* to weep,
And old *re-morse* meant being bitten twice,
And why the soul in tears' container steep?

Far better gently touch the flaws that sleep
And label each in manner gentle, nice.
Repent is linked to pain, *regret* to weep,

But why not mild infractions overleap?
And why subject a child to ill device?
And why the soul in tears' container steep

That him in brine-keg deep immersed might keep?
To heal, my superego grieved entice!
Repent is linked to pain, *regret* to weep.

A cooler Buddhist mood will let you sweep
Vain care aside, not eat the bitter spice.
And why the soul in tears' container steep?

Whatever woe we sow indeed we'll reap.
So let it go, let be, is my advice.
Repent is linked to pain, *regret* to weep,
And why the soul in tears' container steep?

Thoughts on "The diabetic takes a daily test"

There's a light-hearted whimsy about this villanelle: I'm quick to accentuate the positive and dismiss all "dule" or dolor, grief—or even worry.

But I have to admit something. More than a bit of pride sneaked in, as if the partly self-directed sermonette were meant to be a self-portrait of one who followed his own advice with rigor and was therefore content.

The fact is that the adjurations aren't easy to follow unless you're on the watch for self-deception. And the pleasure-seeking id is guileful, sly.

Not long ago my regularly tabulated sugar level ratings began to rise, and it turned out I needed a new medicinal supplement. The dosage was only 5 mg. per day, but the improvement was quick and remarkable.

During the next four-month trial period after the cheerful result was conveyed to the doctor, the sugar level began to sneak up again. My thought was: Why be concerned? Most likely, another daily 5 mg. mini-dose will do the trick.

It wouldn't. The doctor doubled the dose of my main medication instead. Startled, I asked him if this would really take care of the matter. He replied, "Only if you also do more exercise and reduce caloric intake. The medicine will work if these things are done." The unviability of my "most likely" optimism tactic was unmasked.

I do have a strong will though, when I resolve to use it. *Ad astra per aspera!*

81 The diabetic takes a daily test

The diabetic takes a daily test
As might a student in a well-run school.
Behave yourself. See better change to best.

By scientific findings are we blest:
We have the pills, we're taught the helpful rule.
The diabetic takes a daily test

Of scooping knowledge from the treasure chest,
For it is there, and he is not a fool:
Behave yourself. See better change to best.

Who eat high-protein bread will soon arrest
The carbo harm and feel the vanished dule.
The diabetic takes a daily test

And, ever student on a learning quest,
Longevity might earn with finer fuel.
Behave yourself. See better change to best.

Don't eat too much, but give the belly rest.
Be disciplined—you'll ease both pee and stool.
The diabetic takes a daily test:
Behave yourself. See better change to best.

Thoughts on "I feel the urge to sing, but—what of this?"

Not a tech whiz, I used to be apprehensive about the weekly changes of Windows 10 365. New mechanical adaptations thoughout the year, to be learned on a weekly basis? By someone with a divergent eye focus who'd always had certain problems with physical space?

But imagination led me far astray with nervous fear that all proved pointless. Many of the changes are small, or even unnoticeable by the computer typer, and many have considerably lightened my tasks, particularly in quoting foreign languages.

There was, and is, no tech problem. What had misled me for awhile was an imagination problem. William Blake (1757–1827) writes:

Eternity
He who binds to himself a joy
Does the winged life destroy;
But he who kisses the joy as it flies
Lives in eternity's sun rise.

Fear of the future is the villain in all Blake's epic poems, for it generates a mentality of clutching, grabbing what you've got and never letting go. That's a miserly attitude, and the miser will be miserable. Open-mindedness = openness to time's flight, to the sunrise of new experience that William Wordsworth called "something evermore about to be" (*The Prelude* VI.542).

82 I feel the urge to sing, but—what of this?

I feel the urge to sing, but—what of this?
Let Windows 10 its Thursday update make:
I'm lent a lesson that I cannot miss.

When things don't change, the calm appears a
    bliss,
But, asked to alter, pray don't umbrage take.
I feel the urge to sing, but—what of this?

You're kept alert—your thinking won't dehisce
Nor let delay the neural system shake:
I'm lent a lesson that I cannot miss.

Not thing but *service*—your computer. Kiss
The "permanent" farewell, resurge, awake!
I feel the urge to sing, but—what of this?

Improvement aiding, praise, and never hiss:
More tranquil than the surface of a lake,
I'm lent a lesson that I cannot miss.

Remaining static—what a huge abyss!
In sunrise rather live, said William Blake.
I feel the urge to sing, but—what of this?
I'm lent a lesson that I cannot miss.

Thoughts on "Depict the moments from within: you'll know them more"

In thoughts about poem 79 I referred to the "phenomenology" of Edmund Husserl, the discipline of attending to the structure of what appears to you

To concentrate on what's happening to your face when a neutral expression turns into a smile is a joy beyond the smile itself. Movements of the musculature are the wonder explored in tercet 1.

With tercet 2 we focus on how the eyes are changing in their new emotion, followed by an unexpected feeling of what strong movement the jaws were making.

Every stage of the observing of a smile is a distinct delight, and as the moments or factors are felt to blend the joy will grow.

Is it true that my earholes widened, too? Is it verifiable that a snowdrift will exhibit tints of orange, blue, or pink? Try the smile yourself, look at the snow, test out everything. The making of a "phenomenology of daily [or momently] life" is up to you. It will be the savoring of gifts that were bestowed unknown.

The final quatrain tells of the pleasure that comes from writing up the results in metered harmony, in verse. The widened eyes and earholes instantiate in the most vividly concrete of ways what William Blake meant by saying, in *The Marriage of Heaven and Hell* (1793), "If the doors of perception were cleansed everything would appear to man as it is, Infinite."

83 Depict the moments from within: you'll know them more

Depict the moments from within: you'll know them more.
Just now I felt: to be alive—how fine that sense!
I smiled and felt each muscle, could their might explore.

The eyes—I felt them brighten, and delight outpour:
The motions of the jaw were tightened, yet not tense.
Depict the moments from within: you'll know them more.

There can't be any ranking of the minutes, for
They each contain united human elements.
I smiled and felt each muscle, could their might explore:

It even seemed my earholes widened, each a door
To waken my awareness of a thought immense.
Depict the moments from within: you'll know them more,

Then tell the world what you have learned. No hoarder or
Mere self-enclosed unfortunate, fear no expense.
I smiled and felt each muscle, could their might explore.

How loved, at length, the possibility to soar
Illumed in lore of heaven-tune descended thence!
Depict the moments from within: you'll know them more:
I smiled and felt each muscle, could their might explore.

Thoughts on "A part of what enabled me to sing"

The *Arabian Nights* tells of Aladdin, whose magic ring could conjure up a genie, as could the more famous magic lamp he had. The genies of the lamp and ring play roles both alternating and combined in saving Aladdin from cunning plots and wiles of ill-wishers.

A lamp is a more fast-acting symbol of "enlightenment," but a ring helps me focus on what I care for in this poem. The rhythms of 4, 5, or 6 beats that I use in villanelles are recurrent, and the ouroboros, or snake with tongue in its mouth, presents the ring of perpetual recurrence.

The rhymes and word harmonies of recurrent vowels or consonants offer another, audible kind of ring. Especially when refrains are prominent, the repeated adages or proverbial-sounding lines may ring vibrantly in the mind and be remembered.

It can't be accidental that the writer often reputed as perhaps the best ever, my friend William with whom I exchanged sonnets in *Shakespair* (2015), wrote so many thousands of iambic pentameters.

In grade school, teachers told us, "Don't read poetry in a sing-song way, read it as if you were reading a normal book or article, and don't stop at the ends of lines, but just go on in a totally natural way." If that happens, the rhythm will be annihilated and the "immortal" Shakespeare will die the death. Poetic elocution, the art of reading poetry in a way that blends normal speech patterns with subtle changes of emphasis to make us hear the beat, can revive my comrade.

84 A part of what enabled me to sing

A part of what enabled me to sing
The tiniest arousal of my day
Is merely the iambic magic ring—

No splashy glitz, no dazzle-flashy bling,
A casual, relaxing language-way—
A part of what enabled me to sing

The simplest or most complicated thing.
The key to what in chant I'd want to say
Is merely the iambic magic ring.

It has an easy, rangy amble-swing
That's made the walking work a gentle sway,
A part of what enabled me to sing.

Its heart-beat rhythm that, when on the wing,
Each cloud can penetrate with eagle-play
Is merely the iambic magic ring

That with Aladdin-glad imagining
I rub and upward over hilltop stray.
A part of what enabled me to sing
Is merely the iambic magic ring.

Thoughts on "What Swinburne called a nympholept am I"

A corybant is a wild, frenzied worshiper or priestess of Cybele, Phrygian nature goddess, and "nympholept" is a word that arose from Greek roots in the 18th century to denote anyone in a similar seizure by the unknown, unseen, and longed for.

"Sing in me, Muse," the request made by Homer at the beginning of his *Odyssey*, formed part of a polite conversation, as indeed the hero speaks casually with his patroness Athena during her casual visitings throughout the book. But I need something wilder and less confined to bring across the unrelenting strength of the poetry impulsion. A day is oddly incomplete when I can't make a lyric verse at my machine, the Promethean computer powered by transoceanic sparks (and I do like to send my poems flying over the waters at more than lightning speed to friends in Europe).

The music depicted here happens when the heart is touched by the drum of rhythm and by the flute and "barbiton" (= lute) that can represent the Dionysian and Apollonian, the chaotic and calm expressions of the godly urge.

The singer, ascending to heaven and then descending as the dew, is like Muhammad (in the rise) and like the mercy of Allah (in the falling-down) to the prostrate reciter of "The Opening" who greets the dawn.

The fawn is a pastoral emblem but also recalls the goat-like satyr-fauns of Greek myth, spirits of fertility.

85 What Swinburne called a nympholept am I

What Swinburne called a nympholept am I
When by the wild command swept up and on,
Who nothing hear but corybant's wild cry.

Two villanelles ago, you'd startled spy
A hexametric beat mere drive might spawn.
What Swinburne called a nympholept am I.

I didn't know I'd switch from fives. And why?
So wished the muse that summoned me at dawn
Who nothing hear but corybant's wild cry.

Well kens the mind the heart will never lie:
She touches drum and flute and barbiton.
What Swinburne called a nympholept am I.

To height of heaven-rune I first would fly,
Descending then to rose on dewy lawn,
Who nothing hear but corybant's wild cry.

Though born of earth I seek the morning sky.
No leaf more blest than I, that feeds the fawn.
What Swinburne called a nympholept am I,
Who nothing hear but corybant's wild cry.

Thoughts on "To seek the most arousing way to read"

Rather than "speed reading" I plead for slow. The eye has nothing to do with the joy of singable verse. The best literary hoax in history is the poems of "Ossian," claimed to be the first discoveries of *Fragments of Ancient Poetry* (1760), Gaelic survivals, but really written by James Macpherson. He printed them as if they were prose. But that fooled no one! I'll print lines, from page 14, in verse format:

Returnest thou safe from the war?
Where are thy friends, my love?
I heard of thy death on the hill;
I heard and mourned thee, Shilric.

Yes, my fair, I return;
But I alone of my race.
Thou shalt see them no more:
Their graves I raised on the plain.
But why art thou on the desert hill?
Why on the heath, alone?

Alone I am, O Shilric!
Alone in the winter-house.
Shilric, I am pale in the tomb.

She's a ghost. Schubert set this to music: "Allein in der Winterbehausung!" Nearly every line has 3 beats. In other places they may have 4. Pushkin imitated them in Russian, Goethe in German. It was a culture of the audible.

86 To seek the most arousing way to read

To seek the most arousing way to read
The poet's work aloud that you promote
Means care for every word: the rhythm heed

And modulate for slow and rapid speed,
And quantum changes in the feeling note.
To seek the most arousing way to read,

Both intellect and true emotion feed,
And never phrase in vain intone by rote
Means care for every word: the rhythm heed,

That life-resemblance may be guaranteed.
Lord Byron thought of lightly-guided boat,
To seek the most arousing way to read.

Mobility, he urged, is what you need.
A supple instrument, the human throat
Means care for every word: the rhythm heed,

And if your thought-in-song be rightly keyed
A conversation tone will freely float.
To seek the most arousing way to read
Means care for every word: the rhythm heed.

Thoughts on "Came the rehearsal break, I heard the festive bell"

In all the time I've been writing "flash essays" or "blogatelles" for poems, nothing like this ever happened. I can't remember what the refrain was literally about. "Came the rehearsal break, I heard the festive bell"—the sound of it hypnotized me—I was sure I'd never forget the moment. But it's gone ...

And then—why the ocean? Evidently the idea of a "break," a "festive" mood, and a sailor-like departure combined as in a dream to sum up a feeling of being swept away.

One thing is clear: the poetry of J. W. von Goethe was making me feel liberated. The freedom celebration is working in three ways.

First comes the idea of "puberty renewed," Goethe's own phrase ("eine wiederholte Pubertät," *Conversations with Eckermann* March 11, 1828). He felt that lucky people, with resilient entelechies or growth principles, would have these renewals, as he himself did, even into old age. I understand this 100%.

Second, I recalled a song from Goethe's *West-East Divan*, which I had translated. In this pub tune the German poet told us that the name of Mejnoun, the Middle Eastern Romeo, couldn't *really* mean crazy, even though that's what it always did mean. Goethe said he identified too directly with Mejnoun for them both to be called lunatics (see poem 79 in the "Book of Anger" section of his volume). The "mad" lover, exiled by a rival clan from his "Juliet" (Laila), wrote her name repeatedly in the sand, only to watch the holy letters unrelentingly swept away by moving dunes. One whose life has featured recurrent puberties will not condemn him.

87 Came the rehearsal break, I heard the festive bell

Came the rehearsal break, I heard the festive bell
Declaring lyric pleasure I awhile might take:
As ocean traveler I'd glimpse a flowing swell

Of waves that loving tale of dulcet days would tell
Which bard turned twelve years old might yet more
    youthful make.
Came the rehearsal break, I heard the festive bell

Assuring me hexameters would glad compel
The gliding motion that a meter-thirst would slake.
As ocean traveler, I'd glimpse a flowing swell

That, trancing requisite, would work for lover-spell.
So puberty renewed would Goethe's mood awake.
Came the rehearsal break, I heard the festive bell—

Then Persian pub-tune could re-chant what fate
    befell
When human heart, though pressed too hard,
    refused to break.
As ocean traveler, I'd glimpse a flowing swell.

While poor Mejnoun had Laila left for desert hell
Where he her name would write in sand for heaven's
    sake,
Came the rehearsal break, I heard the festive bell:
As ocean traveler, I'd glimpse a flowing swell.

Thoughts on "Inhabiting the lines you're acting out"

Maybe it was the pleasure and craziness of identifying with Goethe and Mejnoun in poem 87 that gave me the feeling of demon and angel co-present in me when I "act out" other identities in imagining. "Mejnoun" isn't a proper name so much as an attribute, an adjective; it is quite likely related to Hebrew/Yiddish *meshugge,* a crazy guy. But he's no more, or less, crazed than Don Quixote. And he's a parable of ardor, therefore of passion, including *furor poeticus,* the poetic madness.

I love to think of the soul as a stem-cell, capable of being proliferated, exfoliated, elaborated into anything at all.

I create a person-of-the-moment every time I write. All writing is acting. Every lyric is a script. On my YouTube of Nikolay Gumilev I shout, laugh, and cry when reciting narratives and monologues by the Russian world traveler poet. It's required—isn't it?—when you're reading soliloquies or legendary tales of the Prodigal Son, Ulysses, Columbus, or the indomitable Ahmed Ogly who intends, despite his "senior" age, to walk to Mecca?

The role played by the speaker of any poem is that of an imagined, therefore fictive "persona." *Persona* is the Latin word for mask, and masks were worn in Greco-Roman tragedy. I like to translate people who don't resemble me at all, or only rather slightly: Esenin the melancholy teenager, Annensky the perpetually aging mentor without a message. When I write a book preface I turn back into the placid professor I used to be, and that everybody thought I must remain.

88 Inhabiting the lines you're acting out

Inhabiting the lines you're acting out
To let potentials hid arise to light
Will make you laugh and cry, be silent, shout.

The angels come—will they the demons rout?
You're showing, twinned, the rival forms of
    might.
Inhabiting the lines you're acting out

You're saint and lover, youth and sage and lout,
O stem-cell of a soul! Plans grown in plight
Will make you laugh and cry, be silent, shout.

The timid who their bravery would tout
Become what they conceive: enchanting sight!
Inhabiting the lines you're acting out,

Entreaty, whisper, tears, or fustian-spout,
If granted by the dream-brain benedight,
Will make you laugh and cry, be silent, shout.

From seedbed-mind will myriad people sprout
That dozed within the luscious loam of night:
Inhabiting the lines you're acting out
Will make you laugh and cry, be silent, shout.

Thoughts on "A program lacking thesis or a plan"

Here's what happened when my colleague Marina Zalesski and I made an hour-and-a-half YouTube of selections, with conversational comment, from the volume of translations I had made, *Russia's World Traveler Poet: Eight Collections by Nikolay Gumilev* (2016). We hadn't rehearsed at all.

I noticed that the way the conversation went suggested the selections that were, on the spot, picked out (though from a list made beforehand). The interaction between the comments and the recitations, by Marina in Russian and by me in English, formed a portrait that took on the unifying theme of "readiness for death."

A virtual essay was being written: it felt so integrated and satisfying that the mood resulting was one of complete fulfilment. It must be how actors feel who have thoroughly appropriated, and been appropriated by, their roles in a play.

Part of the happiness was that of the unpredictable. And, as with most unexpected adventures, there were omissions. The oddest of these, to me, was the complete vanishing of "Drunken Dervish" from my awareness. I had been polishing this poem for years—one of my favorites, but only obliquely related to the theme "readiness for death." Here's how it begins:

In the cypresses are nightingales—the moon begins to
    shine.
Little black stone, little white stone, I have drunk a lot of
    wine.
Than my heartbeat louder far, my bottle melody has made:
"All the world is friendly smiling eyes ashine, the rest but
    shade."

89 A program lacking thesis or a plan

A program lacking thesis or a plan
Save reading from the verse we'd liked or made
New mind-horizon both of us let scan.

We're longtime pedagogues, and thus we can
Some insight, improvised, relaxed unlade.
A program lacking thesis or a plan

Would help the conversation outward fan:
The brave adventurer whom we portrayed
New mind-horizon both of us let scan.

The newly shapen portrait of the man
Rejuvenation brought that cannot fade.
A program lacking thesis or a plan

Gave dreamlike freedom, wider, deeper span
To chance awakings blent of light and shade.
New mind-horizon both of us let scan

Who felt our thought advancing in the van
Of dialogues bilingual grace-arrayed.
A program lacking thesis or a plan
New mind-horizon both of us let scan.

Thoughts on "Each hint you in the shine of eyes can see"

Anyone who has loved teaching will know what I mean by "the shine of eye" revealing "how to reach what you can be." Though we always address everyone, we can't help giving special attention to those who have a receptive gleam of lively interest in their look. You can also observe the bodily gestures—how people move when they wish to hear better or to be closer to the action.

Of course I never can think the thought "vocation" nowadays without reference to my recent reading of Sufi ruminations on the topic. The angel who summons you recites his/her own name, but it will also be yours if you choose to embody the potential it denominates in your own life as a prospective identity.

The eye-gleam student is an angel of this kind. The reactions you elicit by one statement or another can influence what you'll say or think of next. The dialogue of eyes, as much or more than that of words, is a double interpretation of the thought being advanced. Here I have to note that ec-stasy means literally feeling "beside yourself." Two viewpoints are the actors in an expanded drama.

This topic is rooted in what happened to me during the YouTube performance treated in the comments to poems 87 and 88. Not only did I respond to the remarks of my collocutor at the table up front, I was observing reactions from people in the audience, in their words and their expressions.

90 Each hint you in the shine of eye can see

Each hint you in the shine of eye can see
Of thankful hearer helping guide your aim
Will teach you how to reach what you can be.

Past judgment hinders thinking that could free:
'Tis from the sunrise that I hear my Name.
Each hint you in the shine of eye can see

That tells your future, saying, "Come to me"
May well bespeak, unclamoring, what claim
Will teach you how to reach what you can be.

We change more quickly than we think. The fee
Of learning this? Relax, let go self-blame.
Each hint you in the shine of eye can see

Your spirit in a light will bathe which we
Can only gain who give. Soft air aflame
Will teach you how to reach what you can be.

Your Name is calling. Sudden, startlingly,
A starting point is viewed in higher frame:
Each hint you in the shine of eye can see
Will teach you how to reach what you can be.

Thoughts on "The wonder wasn't quite bewilderment"

Repent, remorse, regret, and ruefulness—the time wasters critiqued in my thoughts on poem 80—none of these are here. When Rumi's jealous son Alaeddin kills Shams, his father's treasured friend and spiritual comrade, the "sun" (literal meaning of the name "Shams") did not go out for Rumi. He went to the crafts fair and at the goldsmithing booth encountered—in a musical moment I describe—the next embodiment of that Divine and solar light: Salahuddin Zarkub. Indeed, it was that encounter, which was a joyful whirling dance, that appears to have inspired the poet to found the Whirling Dervishes, who inspire us today.

What may be called the Mentor Faith is concomitant to Rumi's outlook generally. He taught me the guiding metaphor that the Angel Names, rubrics for the perfections that exist forever as potentials among the attributes of God, are that paradoxical wonder, Names That Call You. When you embody such a summoning Name, you become something you didn't know you had it in you to be.

As the Names or Angels are each a mentor, so too we need earthly mentor-friends whom we may love and emulate. Shakespeare's world-famed sonnets, 154 in total, show his love not only for the famed "dark lady" but, even more, for his male friend, the beloved comrade to whom he addresses the first 39 of his love poems in this collection (see my *Shakespair*). Alfred, Lord Tennyson dedicated *In Memoriam*, perhaps the greatest elegy in our language, to his friend Arthur Hallam, who had died at sea. The mystic heights reached by this divine comradeship are not excelled in our literature. In poem 66 and the comment, I have called a Friend the difference between poetry and psychosis. The Mentor Faith may be the first of saving graces.

91 The wonder wasn't quite bewilderment

The wonder wasn't quite bewilderment.
When Rumi's son dear Shams, fine Friend, had slain
He wouldn't cry. He had a high intent.

The folk were baffled, yet a lesson lent
To them in this would be: why nourish pain?
The wonder wasn't quite bewilderment

When they observed how quickly Rumi went
To see the gemcraft-goldsmith fair. 'Twas plain
He wouldn't cry. He had a high intent.

The clinking hammers (gamelans?) were blent
In harmony of spheres—a holy fane!
The wonder wasn't quite bewilderment—

But heaven-bliss! The booth, by tones besprent,
Would Rumi's newer questing-Friend contain.
He wouldn't cry. He had a high intent:

To whirl with comrade-soul from heaven sent.
So dervishes yet whirl, whom none constrain.
The wonder wasn't quite bewilderment:
He wouldn't cry. He had a high intent.

Thoughts on "The night of quietude, my friend"

Poetry itself may be a mentor-friend of the kind I described in the thoughts on poem 91. And at night, my writing time, the friendship is felt and celebrated with intensity and joy. In my final quatrain I compare the withdrawn or "sundered sun" to a "jewel," an allusion to the friendly dance-encounter when poet Rumi met the new "Shams," the mentor-sun who succeeded the comrade that had just died, a meeting that took place among the goldsmiths at the jewelers' fair.

The memories of Rumi that hovered in mind while I wrote this poem help explain the archaic words "dule" (dolor, grief, woe) and "wight" (person), for poetic archaisms bring into feeling the realm of legend, the freeing-time of dream at night. The "night of quietude" expends brisk and chilly air to cleanse, invigorate, and purify the spirit so that tired truths may be "left at school" and that we may also leave the entry-hall or "vestibule" of day to enter the royal chambers of the Palace, even to see the Throne.

"Lo! the vigil of the night is (a time) when impression is more keen and speech more certain" (Qur'an 73:6). The Prophet Muhammad loved the night so much that often he stayed up late to pray and couldn't find the strength for the five required devotions on the day following. But he is pardoned for this readily excusable weariness, brought on by liking for the keener perceiving and greater vigor in speech that the night affords (for the modern poet as for him). "Lo! thy Lord knoweth how thou keepest vigil sometimes nearly two-thirds of the night, or sometimes half, or a third thereof. ... Recite then, of the Qur'an, that which is easy for you" (73:20).

92 The night of quietude, my friend

The night of quietude, my friend,
The time of tranquil earth and cool—
To her my heart do I commend.

The air-embrace I feel extend
To shelter me from threat and dule—
The night of quietude, my friend,

The wealth of brisk and chill may spend,
That freedom rise and dream-world rule—
To her my heart do I commend.

The facts that proud we thought we kenned
Are glad outgrown and left at school.
The night of quietude, my friend,

Declares I, willing wight, may wend
Beyond the daytime vestibule:
To her my heart do I commend,

The art-realm thus to comprehend
Where sundered sun becomes a jewel.
The night of quietude, my friend—
To her my heart do I commend.

Thoughts on "Unconscious cowing by authorities"

It starts early and goes on late: report card, diploma, journal peer review, press editor, salary committee continue to rate you by the year and by the decade. Retired now for thirteen years (a time when I've published 18 poetry books with a number of scholarly prefaces), I still have dreams of having failed to do this or that, to be here or there, to fulfill one or another obligation. So poem 93, a self-directed sermonette, is lyric therapy addressed to the undying little child inside who never stops feeling he'd better get straight A's. The "maxim planted on the page," made at least "brave in phrasing," may be heard, one hopes, by fearful jinns within the id that far too long was timid.

The problem, unconscious cowing by authorities that have taken up residence in the dream-world, must be widespread, as the phone calls I receive can show. Yesterday I got a call from "Joe," at the "Department of the Treasury," telling me that unspecified crimes would bring down major penalties upon my head unless I called his number to get the matter rectified. Later the same day, "Nancy" reinforced the importance of the unknown alleged misdeed by repeating the threat in other phrasings and giving me, again, a salutiferous number to contact. The scammers think the inner child may be readily terrified and terrorized.

Reporters reveal these frauds, making it clear that scams capitalizing on older folks' childish dream-fears can be called a national phenomenon. We need to learn, early on, that we're alive not in order to gratify someone's "expectations," or to work "for" someone (see poem 98). A human "being" can only "be" when setting its own goals, working for its own potential.

93 Unconscious cowing by authorities

Unconscious cowing by authorities,
Defeating so the bright advance of years,
Uncured may lend the older soul unease.

The maxim planted on the page can please
And, brave in phrasing, heal the mind that fears
Unconscious cowing by authorities.

'Tis wearying, this paying of the fees
Exacted by a lack of faith. Past jeers
Uncured may lend the older soul unease.

Let warming light make friends of enemies!
For calm's the inner fire. Away it clears
Unconscious cowing by authorities.

The drive in me by god imparted sees
The far horizon-life: no vision-blears
Uncured may lend the older soul unease.

Strong heart is at the root of art that frees:
With outward rays reply to inward spears.
Unconscious cowing by authorities
Uncured may lend the older soul unease.

Thoughts on "Said Enterpriser to the Undertaker"

The life story that I write by living owes plenty to the Romantic poets of the later 18th and early 19th centuries. Three of them are highlighted, though unnamed, in these 19 short lines.

Johann Wolfgang von Goethe (1749–1832), Germany's greatest poet, has already appeared in lyrics 13, 17, 19, 28, 62, 86, 87, and 88. In #87 I introduced his feeling, and ideal, of a "recurrent puberty." My third life is better called resilience than retirement. Youth Renewable is the Enterpriser's motto of protest to the Undertaker.

William Wordsworth (1770–1850), is our language's most renowned celebrator of Mother Earth. His verse autobiography is called *The Prelude*, but as it unfolds we note that the prelude was the time of child-and-earth daily inter-allied in the rural environs of Grasmere, as much through fear and awe as through delight and comfort: his tale of childhood is the narrative of the force that, tranquilly recollected, resurges in all the lasting poems he wrote. This revival ties in with my Goethe theme of recurrent puberty.

George Gordon, Lord Byron (1788–1824) portrays himself in *Childe Harold* as imaginatively blended with the fictional Harold and the larger-than-life Napoleon in one threefold image of a Promethean fire-spirit uncontrolled and ungovernable. One has to dare the unattempted, while yet nourished by the imaginative past as are the holy courtyard trees in Psalm 92:12–13.

94 Said Enterpriser to the Undertaker

Said Enterpriser to the Undertaker,
"Hold off awhile, third life I want to lead:
Child, grownup, poet, here's a threefold Maker."

Each day I'm granted, I'm a value staker—
Juvescent, jubilant, new-pubertied!"
Said Enterpriser to the Undertaker.

"In vim prolific, who's the record breaker?
Who better to advise, and guide to speed?
Child, grownup, poet, here's a threefold Maker,

Re-juiced, in courtyard of the Lord a Waker:
The righteous palm, the cedar me will heed!"
Said Enterpriser to the Undertaker.

"A nature singer, latter Grasmere Laker,
I chant of Mother, who our souls doth feed:
Child, grownup, poet, here's a threefold Maker,

And, Byron-like, I'll be a heaven-shaker
When called to prove the maxim by the deed,"
Said Enterpriser to the Undertaker,
"Child, grownup, poet, here's a threefold Maker."

Thoughts on "Let's overtake the poet world by storm"

Pre-Freudian Plato gave us, in *Phaedrus,* an allegory of the human as a charioteer with two steeds, Reason and Passion (superego and id, perhaps) that cause problems when they run at different speeds. Balancing the two impulsions can be a major feat, but Plato attempts, we might say, to please both Passion and Reason in his supplementary dialogue, *Symposium*, which means "drinking party" Here he tells us that Love is a ladder with steps or gradations, leading from the love of beautiful bodies to that of beautiful minds, and next to that of beautiful ideas, with the most beautiful of all ideas being that of Beauty itself, which leads us to Virtue, as well, and to experience both of them as one with Knowledge.

The Prophet Muhammad is affirmed in the hadith or memoir-narrative literature to have been supernaturally transported from Mecca to Jerusalem. In legend he travels on the back of a winged, steed-like creature named Buraq, or Lightning. (She has a womanly face, and one can see pictures of the white horse-like animal with a lovely female visage on trucks in Pakistan today.) It is also told that Muhammad toured the heavenly spheres and at last contemplated a vision of God. Often he has been pictured as making this journey, too, astride Buraq.

Plato's Beauty-Virtue-Knowledge and Muhammad's Heaven are reached, to put it roughly, on horseback, and even in these modern times when we no longer picture a person of noble achievement as a cavalier, chevalier, caballero, or other horseman, a supernal mood may come from the thunder-beat of distant approaching hooves. Thus we "overtake the poet world by storm."

95 Let's overtake the poet world by storm

Let's overtake the poet world by storm:
The horses of the night let loose, we ride
Above the chaos to the height of Form.

Muhammad rode the steed sublime, the norm
Of Prophet-spell as he to heaven hied.
Let's overtake the poet world by storm:

Though Plato-steeds unequally perform
They both to one same wisdom rein are tied.
Above the chaos to the height of Form

We're going, whom the brighter sun can warm,
For we the charger may with practice guide:
Let's overtake the poet world by storm—

Blest heart of bard with honey-tones aswarm—
Enrapt, the chanter, in a light espied—
Above the chaos, to the height of Form!

Deep-stored below in bulbo-tuber corm,
Spring nutriment the winter chill defied.
Let's overtake the poet world by storm:
Above the chaos, to the height of Form!

Thoughts on "The hero and the minstrel may unite"

Peg Weiss' volume *Kandinsky and Old Russia: The Artist as Ethnographer and Shaman* was a treasure world of new experience for me, and the first of my tercets will tell you why. The shaman (called "medicine man" in the antiquated books of my childhood) is at once priest, prophet, and deliverer. The drum he beats while telling his tale becomes the horse on which he rides while acting it out, the "actor and the chanter being one." The tale is a play with one performer. We can't call it merely a dramatic monologue, for it contains confrontation and exchange between the chanter and the demons he must overcome. The drama is therapeutic, for the troubling spirits are within, and the result is a work of art in lyrical meter: thus "The hero and the minstrel may unite."

The privileged "dreamer-hearing" of the visionary rider stuns the spirit-forces whose rebel cries he takes in and then dispels in the deliverance-plot he is acting out. When I say our hero "ravels out what fate has spun" I'm aware of the jostling rival meanings of the wonder-word "ravel": to untangle and to entangle, as threads get tangled when they're unwoven. I hint that "fate" or "destiny" or any other spirit-pretender that wants or claims control of your life needs a counteracting push in the healing process. That push is your freedom, and the shaman achieves it through artistic will.

Greek Bellerophon rode the winged steed Pegasus on his way to Mount Olympus, Prophet Muhammad in Islam is often pictured (in Shi'a paintings) astride the horse-like creature Buraq ("Lightning") on his way through the heavens to God. Shaman drum-steed offers godly flight.

96 The hero and the minstrel may unite

The hero and the minstrel may unite,
The actor and the chanter being one
If shaman on the drum-steed should alight.

To drumming-horse, the spirit foe we fight
Will shout! We, voicing him, on verse-track run.
The hero and the minstrel may unite

As we in dialogue can set things right
By letting speakers dreamer-hearing stun.
If shaman on the drum-steed should alight

And guide the creature with his vocal might
He freely ravels out what fate had spun:
The hero and the minstrel may unite

And glory-verse warm passion thus requite
Until the journey to the gods be done!
If shaman on the drum-steed should alight

No fetter keeps him from the heaven-height—
O fierce the joy of conquest, and the fun!
The hero and the minstrel may unite
If shaman on the drum-steed should alight.

Thoughts on "I join the fingertips of left and right"

A doctor once told me I had the "most left-centered body" he had ever seen: everything on my left side is bigger. Wondering what this might mean, I've read a number of articles about left-handedness, but there's much disagreement concerning it. The most invigorating because apparently best balanced presentation of the topic argued that we should regard the trait as an evolutionary experiment. Nature is trying something out, to see how it will work when combined with other options.

What I enjoy about it is the minority status it gives me. Freud, in one of several biographies of him that I've read (for he's one of my heroes), made the claim that, despite his lack of belief, being Jewish had helped him advance in life and work. It had accustomed him to view things from a minority viewpoint and encouraged his freedom from opinions accepted by some majority or other.

Left-handedness is like that. I never saw a left-handed shirt in a clothing store: the pocket would be on the right side of the shirt so the left hand could reach it. When I was young, desk-chair units were always arranged so a right-handed person could rest the forearm on an area extending from the desk. Double doors to a room in a business establishment will often have one of the doors permanently locked, and of course it's always the door that a lefty tries to open.

My minority lefty status might be helping me write this book. As poetic lines nowadays get looser and prosier, I look for intricate musical forms, in order to make them more intricate still.

97 I join the fingertips of left and right

I join the fingertips of left and right,
My hands in Dürer's prayer pose aligned,
And note an oddity that came to light:

I find it hard to lend them equal might
Within the touch-perception of the mind.
I join the fingertips of left and right:

My brain is leftward-based and so will fight.
The right-reaction dulled, the will is blind—
And note an oddity that came to light:

I need to feel the left as master, quite!
To think of right-strength—oh, so hard I find ...
I join the fingertips of left and right

But rightward-equalizing thought, despite
My effort, with the leftward's uncombined.
And note an oddity that came to light:

My trying's not entirely vain—the bright
Beginning partnership's not *all* declined. ...
I join the fingertips of left and right
And note an oddity that came to light.

Thoughts on "Place all your expectations where you will"

Deciding you don't "work for" a company, a university, an overlord, or even a higher self unless you feel like doing these things won't make you free. You'll need to ask whether you're "working for" a cultural ideal that is arbitrarily made popular or propagandized in a constraining period of history.

That said, let me leave the rest of the page blank, so you can fill in whatever Name(s) the Awaking Angel may suggest, in daylight or in dreamnight, for you to consider and perhaps adopt.

98 Place all your expectations where you will

Place all your expectations where you will,
Not asking others what they ought to be,
And self-declared requirement then fulfill.

"I work for so-and-so ...."? A bitter pill
To have to take, but—no! I work for *me*.
Place all your expectations where you will:

Your job is not to stuff employers' till.
Think who you are, and what you'd joy to see—
And self-declared requirement then fulfill.

Why be like blinded Samson at the mill?
Runes Odin knew, although half-blinded he ...
Place all your expectations where you will

And higher goal in lower soul instill.
Self-sacrifice, if chosen, force will free
And self-declared requirement then fulfill.

The pilgrim wise may climb the highest hill.
Self-realizing seed becomes a tree.
Place all your expectations where you will
And self-declared requirement then fulfill.

Thoughts on "Fall trees, pure red, rich orange, come to seem"

Rumi—dependable mentor and eternal friend! In poems 56, 77, 78 and the accompanying thoughts, I invoked his waking dream of cosmic life as a flaming round dance, a dervish whirl of fire, and in my favorite season, autumn (where I see the AUtMn hiding), the metaphor comes to life in the Vestal region where I'm privileged to live.

Spending an autumnal month in Germany once, I didn't observe such an arboreal rush of energies unloosed in the flamboyance of approaching age. I need the image as an emblem of my third life.

The colors and the vigor are what make a torch flare wildly in the gusty wind. In letters, the poet Keats hinted at an aesthetic of "gusto," which in its root is a "tasting." Rumi said life must be tasted; he praised few philosophers but lauded Plato, the only one of them who he thought had truly tasted what he lived. I remember a Muslim sage who said that the pleasure of loving God compares with earthly pleasure as sex to sugar. Wine is emblematic, for Sufis, of every kind of love: for a mortal, for the Deity, for the frenzy of poetic ardor.

Leaves in fall are fiery in color and dance-like in movement. The wind that impels them, breathed deeply, can be tasted. The spirit or breath of wind appears embodied in the flying leaves, while the hills with their yellow, red, and orange boughs lift arms upward in a solemn joy. It can be called the shofar trumpet of the resurrection of the breath in gusto. All beings of the world, ensouled with autumn AUM, are conflagrant, conclamant in their burst of hymn and psalm.

99 Fall trees, pure red, rich orange, come to seem

Fall trees, pure red, rich orange, come to seem
A thing predictable as it could be—
A bright delirium, a heaven dream

When we consider: What we normal deem,
A foreigner might find quite strange to see.
Fall trees, pure red, rich orange, come to seem

Most odd where no such fiery wonders teem:
No gingko, linden flames, no German tree.
A bright delirium, a heaven dream,

The leaves new-blazing that in sunray gleam
Are dressed in festal garb with Vestal glee.
Fall trees, pure red, rich orange, come to seem

To vary one essential Rumi theme—
A huge conflagrant world-epiphany,
A bright delirium, a heaven dream.

Though chill the morning, warmth in wind astream
Will glow, and touch the heart, the core of me:
Fall trees, pure red, rich orange, come to seem
A bright delirium, a heaven dream.

Thoughts on "Cease not imagining what yet can be"

A collegial friend and I retired in the same year, and we were fêted together at an English Department dinner. The speaker for the occasion hazarded a contrast.

"Let me draw my parallels from the King Arthur legend," she said. "Frank is like Arthur, the clear-eyed organizer, goal formulator, manager of the kingdom. Things go well when he is in charge, for he combines insight with practicality, and he gets along well with people." Fine words, and fitting, to depict a worthy administrator and tireless helper.

"Martin is different," she went on. "What he wants is to burst into the room showing you something new and unheard-of that he has found. He's hoping to dazzle and to startle. He wants to leave you in a condition of marveling and wonderment. In the Round Table story, he is Merlin, the wizard."

Merlin is something of a troublemaker, so in the poem I counterbalance him with a complement in Sir Galahad, a visionary of the grail. But the speaker was right: I like Merlin better. He's more a Sufi dervish, not needing to seek because he finds.

"The sweven done, the swift are feeling free." In other words, when the dream is over, we wake refreshed and ready for a journey. "Polytropos" or "versatile" is a favorite Homeric word for Odysseus, always "turning" in new directions, introducing a new "turn" of events. If he were a poet, it would be a new "turn of speech." And he is "cunning," shrewd, at best a wizard, at lesser levels only a showman. More than to the sailor crew he relates to Athena, his higher self. E-tern-ity has to be a matter of new turns: unbearable to "rest in peace"!

100 Cease not imagining what yet can be

Cease not imagining what yet can be
Though night bequeath a residue of sad:
We turn—are versatile—eternally.

The sweven done, the swift are feeling free.
With fear, success would never have been had:
Cease not imagining what yet can be.

The nomad-souled a pilgrim heaven see:
What's vanished, vanquished since you were a
    lad!
We turn—are versatile—eternally—

And that is why no dreary fate I dree,
Why good whirls high from out the seeming bad.
Cease not imagining what yet can be.

The spray of wave, the winds in autumn spree,
The gold in azure—made the bolder glad.
We turn—are versatile—eternally.

Dear reader, take my hand and look at me,
We're each a Merlin and a Galahad.
Cease not imagining what yet can be:
We turn—are versatile—eternally.

Name Index

Abraham, *xxii*, 92, 106, 134, 154
Achilles, 156
Adam, 41, 104, 156
Aeneas, 104
Ahmed Ogly, 176
Aladdin, 168, 169
Alaeddin, 182
Alexander, 47
Allah, 22, 46, 170
All-tongue, 38
Alpha, 34
Annensky, Innokenty, 176
Aphrodite, 54, 116
Apollo, 89
Apollonia, 170
Archilocus, 98
Ares, 54
Ariana, 153
Aries, 94, 116
Arion, 90
Aristotle, 44, 108
Árjuna, 18, 19
Arthur (King), 200
Asia, 62
Athena, 170

Atman, 18, 19
Aurora, 54

Bacchus, 34, 35
Bachelard, Gaston, *xxiv*, 196
Bacon, Francis, 36
Barrett Browning, Elizabeth, *xxiv*, 101
Bartók, Béla, *xvii*
Bassarid, 128, 129
Beckett, Samuel, 118
Beethoven, *xvii*, 50
Bellerophon, *xxvii*, 192
Berlin, Isaiah, 98
Bernstein, Leonard, 38
Bible, *xviii*, *xxi*, *xxii*, 14, 36, 58, 86
Bidney, David, 52
Biggers, Jonathan, 138
Biggs, E. Power, 138, 139
Bishop, Elizabeth, *xvii*, 64, 65
Blake, William, *xxi*, 4, 30, 36, 46, 56, 57, 164, 166
Borobudur, 94
Boswell, James, 38

Brahman, 18, 19
Brontë, Charlotte, *xxiv*, 92
Buddha, *xx*, 34, 35, 94
Buddhism, 30
Buddhist, *xviii*, *xxvi*, 18, 160, 161
Buraq, 88, 140, 190, 192
Byron, George Gordon, Lord, *xxvii*, 173, 188, 189

Caesar, Julius, 136
Canis Major, 33
Carlyle, Thomas, *xxiv*, 101
Cavalieri, Grace, 8
Cervantes, Miguel de, 154
Chaucer, Geoffrey, 36, 119
Childhood (Tolstoy), 98
Chödrön, Pema, 160
Christ, 35, 104
Christianity, 106
Christians, 140
Civil War, 134
Coleridge, S. T., *xxiv*, 60, 101, 150
Columbus, 176
Corybant, 128, 129, 170, 171
Creator, 80
Cybele, 128, 170
Cyclops, 54

Darwin, Charles, 4
David, 54, 104, 105
Decker, James M., 92
Demogorgon, 62
Devil, 48, 57, 154
Diana, 153
Dionysian, 170
Dionysus, 128

Don Quixote, 154, 176
Dr. Seuss, 64, 86
Dulcinea del Toboso, 154
Dürer, Albrecht, *xxvii*, 195
Dylan, Bob, 46, 68

Earth, 110, 188
Elizabeth (Queen), 153
Emerson, Ralph Waldo, 10, 82, 83, 144
Enterpriser, 188, 189
Eos, 54
Esenin, Sergey, 176
Essential Being, *xix*, *xx*, 2, 22, 30, 58
Esther, 154
Eve, 92, 104

Falstaff, 48, 142, 143
Florio, John, 34
Freud, Sigmund, 48, 50, 194
Freya, 20, 21

Galahad, Sir, 200, 201
Gallic Wars (Caesar), 136, 138
Genius, 92
God, *xix*, *xviii*, *xxiii*, 2, 10, 14, 40, 47, 52, 58, 62, 72, 80, 88, 106, 112, 128, 157
Godot, 118, 119
Goethe, Johann Wolfgang von, *xix*, *xxvii*, 26, 27, 38, 56, 106, 124, 172, 174, 175, 176, 188
Gorky, Arshile, 52
Grimm brothers, 84
Gumilev, Nikolay, *xxvii*, 34, 118, 176, 178

Index 205

Hallam, Arthur, 182
Hamlet, 48, 68, 142, 143
Heine, Heinrich, 28
Hermes, 102
Hindu, *xviii*, 128
Homer, *xxiv*, 26, 27, 42, 54, 90, 104, 146, 147, 170, 200
Horace, 119
Horus, *xix*, 24, 25
Husserl, Edmund, 158, 166

Ibn Arabi, *xviii*, *xx*, *xxii*, 2, 8, 22, 30, 58, 62, 70, 72, 80, 88
Islam, 106, 128, 192
Islamic, *xviii*, 2, 12, 40, 46, 106, 112, 128
Israel, 60, 72, 73
Iuppiter, 12
Ivanov, Vyacheslav, 60
Ives, Charles, 126

Jacob, 10, 60, 72, 73
Jameson, Kay Redfield, 32
Jenghiz Khan, 98, 99
Jerusalem, 56, 88, 140, 190
Jesus, *xx*, 12, 34, 104
Jews, 140
Job, 116
Johnson, Samuel, 38
Jove, 12, 13, 95
Joyce, James, 42
Judaism, 106
Jung, Carl, 56

Kafka, Franz, 114
Kandinsky and Old Russia (Weiss), 192

Kant, Immanuel, 44
Keats, John, 150, 198
Kris, Ernst, 96
Krishna, 18, 19

Laila, *xxvii*, 174, 175
Lightning, 140, 190, 192
Lincoln, Abraham, 134
Locke, John, 36
Lord, 2, 24, 25, 40, 78, 128, 129, 157, 184

Mab (Queen), *xxvi*, 148
Macpherson, James, *xxvii*, 172
Maeve, 148, 149
Mahler, Gustav, 84
Maine Coon Cat, 18
Marduk, 154
Mary, 34, 35
Mecca, 88, 140, 176, 190
Mejnoun, *xxvii*, 174, 175, 176
Mentor Faith, 182
Merlin, 200, 201
Messiah, 92
Milton, John, 36, 56, 60, 104, 119
Mommsen, Katharina, 34
Monet, Claude, 82
Montaigne, Michel de, 34, 82, 158
Mordecai, 154
Moses, 34, 35, 144, 157
Muhammad (Prophet), *xxvi*, *xxvii*, 34, 40, 46, 60, 88, 140, 141, 144, 170, 184, 190, 191, 192

Napoleon, 98, 99, 188
Newton, Isaac, *xix*, 26, 27, 36, 110, 126
Norwegian Forest Cat, 18

Oceanus, 92
Odin, 197
Odysseus, *xxiv*, 54, 90, 104, 200
Omega, 34
Omnipotence, 92
Otto, Rudolf, 60

Pan, 38, 39
Pangloss, 38
Paradise Lost (Milton), 104
Parmenides of Elea, 156
Passion, 20, 56, 190
Passover, 94
Pasternak, Boris, 64
Pater, Walter, *xxiv*, 101
Patterns of Epiphany (Bidney), *xxiv*, 92, 100
Pegasus, 65, 192
Phenomenology, 158, 166
Phidias, 44
Phoebus, 120, 121
Pickthall, Marmaduke, 46
Plato, *xxvii*, 44, 190, 191, 198
Poesia Abscondita, 118
Poincaré, Henri, *xxiii*
Praxiteles, 44
Prodigal Son, 176
Prometheus, 62, 92
Prospero, 120
Pushkin, Alexander, 172

Queen Mab, *xxvi*, 148
Quixano, Alonso, 154

Qur'an, *xviii*, *xix*, 2, 12, 14, 22, 46, 47, 60, 62, 78, 88, 89, 112, 128, 140, 156, 184

Raboy, Asher, 126
Reason, 190
Rilke, Rainer Maria, 60
Roethke, Theodore, *xvii*, 64, 65
Roxanne, 47
Rückert, Friedrich, 66, 84, 85, 86, 114
Rumi, Mevlevi (Mevlana) Shemseddin, *xxiv*, *xxvi*, 112, 113, 114, 156, 157, 182, 183, 184, 198, 199

Sabbath Queen, 24
Salahuddin Zarkub, 182
Samson, 197
Satan, 56, 154
Saturn, 95
Schiller, Friedrich, 50
Schubert, Franz, 119, 172
Shakespeare, John, 94
Shakespeare, William, *xix*, *xxi*, *xxv*, 28, 29, 36, 48, 66, 86, 94, 119, 120, 121, 142, 143, 153, 168
Shaman, 192
Shams, 182, 183
Shaw, (George) Bernard, 82
Shekhinah, 24, 25
Shelley, Percy Bysshe, 60, 62, 150
Socrates, 34, 58, 146, 147
Solomon, 12, 13, 86
Spinoza, Baruch, *xxi*, 52, 53

Index

Steiner, Rudolf, 16
Steinsaltz, Rabbi Adin, 22, 146
Sufi(s), *xviii–xx*, *xxii–xxiii*, 2, 8, 10, 22, 30, 58, 62, 72, 80, 88, 90, 134, 135, 180, 198, 200
Swinburne, Algernon Charles, 171

Taurus, 94, 95, 116
Tennyson, Alfred, Lord, *xxiv*, 101, 182
Thomas, Dylan, *xvii*, *xxi*, 46, 47, 64, 65, 119
Thor, 20, 21
Tiamat, 154
Titans, 92
Tithonus, 54
Tolstoy, Leo, 98, 99
Torah, 89
Trend, 90
Trojan, 36, 104

Ulysses, 27, 105, 176
Undertaker, 188, 189

Venus, 116
Vergil, 26, 104, 105
Virgo, 95
Vishnu, 18
Voltaire, 38

War and Peace (Tolstoy), 98, 99
Weiss, Peg, 192
Whirling Dervishes, *xxiv*, 112, 182
Whitman, Walt, 68, 134, 135
Wilde, Oscar, 82
Windows 10, 164, 165
Womack, Kenneth, 92
Wordsworth, William, *xix*, *xxvii*, 26, 104, 164, 188

Youth Renewable, 188
YouTube, *xxvii*, 118, 176, 178, 180

Zalesski, Marina, *xxvii*, 178
Zalman, Shneur, 22, 146

BOOKS OF ORIGINAL AND TRANSLATED VERSE
BY MARTIN BIDNEY

Series: East-West Bridge Builders

Volume I: *East-West Poetry:*
A Western Poet Responds to Islamic Tradition in Sonnets,
Hymns, and Songs
State University of New York Press

Volume II: J. W. von Goethe, *East-West Divan:*
The Poems, with "Notes and Essays": Goethe's Intercultural Dialogues
(translation from the German with original verse commentaries)
State University of New York Press

Volume III: *Poems of Wine and Tavern Romance:*
A Dialogue with the Persian Poet Hafiz
(translated from von Hammer's German versions,
with original verse commentaries)
State University of New York Press

Volume IV: *A Unifying Light: Lyrical Responses to the Qur'an*
Dialogic Poetry Press

Volume V: *The Boundless and the Beating Heart*
Friedrich Rückert's The Wisdom of the Brahman
Books 1–4 in Verse Translation with Comment Poems
Dialogic Poetry Press

Volume VI: *God the All-Imaginer:*
Wisdom of Sufi Master Ibn Arabi in 99 Modern Sonnets
(with new translations of his Three Mystic Odes,
27 full-page calligraphies by Shahid Alam)
Dialogic Poetry Press

Volume VII: *Russia's World Traveler Poet:*
Eight Collections by Nikolay Gumilev:
Romantic Flowers, Pearls, Alien Sky, Quiver, Pyre, Porcelain Pavilion,
Tent, Fire Column
Translated with Foreword by Martin Bidney
Introduction and Illustrations by Marina Zalesski
Dialogic Poetry Press

Volume VIII: *Six Dialogic Poetry Chapbooks:*
Taxi Drivers, Magritte Paintings, Gallic Ballads,
Russian Loves, Kafka Reactions, Inferno Update
Dialogic Poetry Press

Volume IX: *A Lover's Art: The Song of Songs in Musical English Meters,*
plus 180 Original Love Poems in Reply—A Dialogue with Scripture
Dialogic Poetry Press

Volume X: *A Hundred Villanelles, A Hundred Blogatelles*
Dialogic Poetry Press

Other Books by Martin Bidney

A Hundred Artisanal Tonal Poems with Blogs on Facing Pages:
Slimmed-down Fourteeners, Four-beat Lines,
and Tight, Sweet Harmonies
Dialogic Poetry Press

Shakespair: Sonnet Replies to the 154 Sonnets of William Shakespeare
Dialogic Poetry Press

Alexander Pushkin, *Like a Fine Rug of Erivan: West-East Poems*
(trilingual with audio, co-translated from Russian and
co-edited with Bidney's Introduction)
Mommsen Foundation / Global Scholarly Publications

Saul Tchernikhovsky, *Lyrical Tales and Poems of Jewish Life*
(translated from the Russian versions of Vladislav Khodasevich)
Keshet Press

A Poetic Dialogue with Adam Mickiewicz: The "Crimean Sonnets"
(translated from the Polish, with Sonnet Preface,
Sonnet Replies, and Notes)
Bernstein-Verlag Bonn

Enrico Corsi and Francesca Gambino,
Divine Adventure: The Fantastic Travels of Dante
(English verse rendition of the prose translation
by Maria Vera Properzi-Altschuler)
Idea Publications

[For e-books of verse and works of criticism see martinbidney.com]

Made in the USA
Columbia, SC
13 July 2017